THE WAY OF STILL WATERS

THE WAY OF STILL WATERS

A Codex of Balance and Virtue Harmonized Edition

Robert Hubbard

Amorphous Publishing Guild

Buffalo, NY USA

Symbolic iconography was created by the author, specifically the primary symbols: The Circle of Nine; The Center Flame; The Riverblade emblem.

Disclaimer

The Way of Still Waters is a philosophical and ethical framework inspired by both real-world traditions and fictional narratives. It is not affiliated with, endorsed by, or representative of any organization, spiritual order, or copyrighted franchise referenced within its lineage chapter. All such references remain the intellectual property of their respective creators.

WWW.WAYOFSTILLWATERS.COM

First Printing, 2026
Trade softcover ISBN: 978-1-949818-31-4
eBook ISBN: 978-1-949818-32-1

Amorphous Publishing Guild
Buffalo, New York, USA
www.Amorphous.Press

For Amanda & April

And to all who seek Balance between strength and gentleness, and to every quiet soul who chooses kindness in a world that often forgets its worth.

CONTENTS

BOOK III: LINEAGE OF THE WAY

BOOK IV: THE DOCTOR'S LENS ON THE
WAY OF STILL WATERS

BOOK V: RELATIONAL ETHICS AND
ALTERNATIVE RELATIONSHIP STRUCTURES

THE JOURNEY BEGINS...

FOREWORD

I was not expecting this book. It's not that I thought the author wasn't capable of deep thought, but that the material here reflects a person who has evolved much since we first met at D'Youville College (now "D'Youville University"). Back in the late 1980s, I was a philosophy major; he pursued Computer Science. In some ways, these roles have reversed.

Apart from playing around with martial arts and dating the same young woman (who is still friends with both of us), we ended up doing business together as I unexpectedly entered the world of web design. We took turns being the web host, then he was my server support liaison with the datacenter, then he drifted off to focus on photography. At some point, he and his wife started a Causeplay organization, where people dress up as superheroes and other characters to bring joy to children in hospitals and raise money for charity.

I think it was over that time that I saw the transformation. For so many years, he seemed more of a cynic than a stoic, and had the attitude of a Sith rather than a Jedi. He was the War Doctor at best. The suffering found in life can do that to people, covering their deeper, better selves.

This book was not written by that pessimist persona. The author, his truer self uncovered, has compiled and distilled in these books the noble, the valiant, the fair and true lessons of various traditions, classic and modern. It aims to illuminate pathways of beneficial social and spiritual practice. The reader is not guided to become some caricature of a warrior, but a solidly better person who will live respected, whose death will be regretted, and their integrity remembered.

Now some of the content here may seem strange to most people. This isn't just because they may be unfamiliar with science fiction mythos. Those are, after all, built on the same archetypes as were distilled by Pericles and The Bard. It is the exploration of the nature and implications of non-traditional sexual relationships, polyamory in particular. Such things are outside our current culture's Overton window. It takes an open mind just to read it if you hold tightly to "traditional" attitudes and mores. Yet every aspect of this book employs sound ethical reasoning, even relationships mentioned mostly in whispers, or not at all.

But the heart of this book (books) is to take the best of the author's — and mankind's — experience, and present it concisely for immediate consideration and relevance. It somehow presents the wisdom of sages and ages in outlines and bullet points, without seeming like a mere list of bumper-sticker platitudes. It's not even trying to be a scholastic work deserving of a place in the dusty stacks of a university basement. It just is. It is too simple to be debated, and too familiar to be obtuse. But – almost like Cliff Notes for a book yet to be written – it is a summary of ideas that could be expounded upon and explored by anyone, making it their own.

This work may allow those who consider virtues too abstract to finally find where the tires hit the pavement. You don't need a degree in Philosophy to appreciate it. And so it is my hope that you, the reader, will find it as unexpected and refreshing as I have.

Ken JP Stuczynski
24 December 2025

Amorphous Publishing Guild

INTRODUCTION

For most of my life, certain concepts and ideas seemed to click with me more than others. The ideas of fairness, justice, compassion, and more. Over decades I've read thousands of books and like many of us, tens of thousands of hours of video. In both reality and fiction certain people resonated with me. Across history and story, certain figures echoed the same virtues: clarity, courage, compassion, and a disciplined heart. I've been influenced by the ideas of both Taoism and Stoicism, as well as the Samurai code of Bushido and the Knights code of Chivalry.

What follows is not a "How-To" guide. It's not a "religion", though I feel most of it will fit well within most faiths' teachings and contradict few of them. It is a Codex of The Way of Still Waters. The late martial arts legend Bruce Lee said, "Be Like Water". This approach, exemplified by his martial art philosophy Jeet Kune Do, encourages individuals to be fluid, absorb what is useful from any source, discard what is not, and develop their own unique way rather than rigidly adhering to a single system or tradition. Key principles include authenticity, continuous self-improvement, and the understanding that limitations are often self-imposed.

Taking inspiration from him, "The Way of Still Waters" is a blend of a dozen inspirational influences for the philosopher, the fan, the seeker, the thinker. Thoughts and concepts to consider and perhaps integrate with one's own personal belief systems. It's a guide with ideas to improve your life and the lives of those around you.

It neither judges nor endorses, it simply is.

If you have skimmed through this and thought "What does Spock have to do with Alexander?" or "Is this a geeky fan fiction?" my answer is simple: Read it with an open mind and see where the stream carries you.

Sometimes the current carries you. Sometimes it teaches you to swim.

Come walk The Way of Still Waters with me and see where your current carries you.

Robert Hubbard
Grandmaster, The Way of Still Waters.
Guardian of the Quiet Flame.

"BECOMING YOURSELF IS A LIFELONG UNFOLDING."

BOOK I: THE WAY OF STILL WATERS

"LIGHT BEGINS AS A DECISION LONG BEFORE IT BECOMES A SUNRISE."

I. ESSENCE AND VISION

STEEL IN VIRTUE — WATER IN MOTION — BALANCE IN WISDOM

The Way of Still Waters is a path of right living — a fusion of Stoic firmness and Taoist flow, shaped by the disciplined traditions of Samurai, Knights, Rangers, and Seekers throughout history. It teaches that calm is not passivity and strength is not rigidity; both arise from harmony, discernment, and right timing.

To live The Way is to act with courage, relate with compassion, and see with clarity —

To be steel when duty calls, and water when wisdom whispers.

The Way holds that every moment offers a choice between force and flow, between impulse and intention.

Steel provides direction, but without Water it becomes unyielding.

Water provides grace, but without Steel it becomes shapeless.

Balance is the quiet center where both qualities meet, allowing the practitioner to move through the world with purpose instead of reaction.

The vision of The Way is not to create warriors or sages, but whole human beings — grounded in virtue, gentle in conduct, and clear in perception. It asks for neither perfection nor purity, only the steady willingness to refine oneself, to return to stillness when scattered, and to act from conscience rather than convenience.

The heart of The Way is simple:

Live with integrity, walk with compassion, and choose courage where fear would rule.

In doing so, the practitioner becomes a calm presence in a turbulent world — guided, not by force or pride, but by the quiet strength of inner clarity.

II. THE CODEX OF RIGHT CONDUCT

"HONOR IN THOUGHT. TRUTH IN WORD. COURAGE IN DEED."

This is the central law — the living heart of The Way.

Everything else in the Codex flows from these three essential directives, which govern the inner life, the spoken life, and the lived life of every practitioner.

HONOR IN THOUGHT

Cultivate integrity within; all conduct begins in the unseen.

Thought shapes intention, intention shapes action, and action shapes the world.

Honor in thought means keeping one's inner landscape free of deceit, malice, and self-betrayal.

It is the quiet discipline of aligning one's motives with virtue before any outward choice is made.

TRUTH IN WORD

Speak with clarity, kindness, and conviction.

Words are the bridges between inner truth and outer action.

Truth in word requires honesty without cruelty, clarity without arrogance, and silence when speaking would cause needless harm. A practitioner's word is a reflection of their character; therefore, speech must flow cleanly, like water unclouded.

COURAGE IN DEED

Act rightly, even when the outcome is uncertain or the path is difficult.

Courage in deed does not require fearlessness — only the willingness to act despite fear.

It demands ethical action when it is easier to remain silent, compassionate action when it is easier to turn away, and steadfast action when virtue requires effort or risk.

These three — **Honor, Truth, and Courage** — mirror the threefold essence of **Steel, Water, and Balance**:

- Honor arises from Balance, the clarity of an aligned inner self.

- Truth flows like Water, shaping the world gently but persistently.

- Courage expresses the strength of Steel, firm and clean in action.

Together, they form the core of the practitioner's conduct — a simple creed that carries profound weight, guiding every choice along The Way of Still Waters.

III. THE THREE CURRENTS

Each Current represents a mode of mastery: **Action, Relationship, and Awareness** — forming a triune discipline of life and leadership.

STEEL — STRENGTH WITH INTEGRITY (RIGHT ACTION)

When the task is yours to do, stand firm and act cleanly. Steel represents **Courage, Duty,** and **Honor** — the virtues of right action.

"Steel acts when silence would cost the innocent."

- **Courage**: Act rightly despite fear; the heart's steel, steady under strain.
- **Duty**: Fulfill what is yours to do, cleanly and without resentment.
- **Honor**: Let your outer deeds mirror your inner truth; dignity through consistency.

WATER — STRENGTH THROUGH FLOW (RIGHT RELATIONSHIP)

When control dissolves, yield and shape the current. Water represents **Compassion, Courtesy,** and **Temperance** — the virtues of right relationship.

"Water moves mountains by patience, not pressure."

- **Compassion**: Empathy made real through care and protection.
- **Courtesy**: Grace in motion; kindness expressed through form.

- **Temperance**: Use only the force required; gentleness is endurance in disguise.

⚖ BALANCE — STRENGTH THROUGH CLARITY (RIGHT AWARENESS)

Between force and flow lies discernment — knowing when to be which. Balance represents **Integrity, Wisdom,** and **Humility** — the virtues of right awareness.

"Balance sees without forcing, and moves without haste."

- **Integrity**: Wholeness between word, thought, and deed.
- **Wisdom**: Know when to be steel, when to be water.
- **Humility**: Remember your place within the greater current.

IV. THE NINEFOLD VIRTUES

Each Current holds three virtues, forming a complete circle of mastery — action refined by compassion, relationship refined by discipline, and awareness refined by clarity.

Current	Virtues	Essence
Steel	Courage • Duty • Honor	Right Action
Water	Compassion • Courtesy • Temperance	Right Relationship
Balance	Integrity • Wisdom • Humility	Right Awareness

THE NINEFOLD CIRCLE

1. **Courage begins action.**
   Without the first step, no virtue can manifest.
2. **Duty sustains it.**
   Commitment carries the work beyond convenience.
3. **Honor completes it.**
   Action gains dignity only when it aligns with truth.
4. **Compassion softens the edge.**
   Strength becomes safe when guided by empathy.
5. **Courtesy guides the motion.**
   Grace shapes interactions, even in difficulty.
6. **Temperance keeps proportion.**
   Restraint ensures that force never becomes excess.
7. **Integrity aligns all parts.**
   Word, thought, and deed become one.
8. **Wisdom selects timing.**
   Right action depends as much on *when* as on *what*.
9. **Humility restores stillness.**
   Ego dissolves, and the practitioner returns to clarity.

"Thus the blade and the stream become one: firm in virtue, fluid in form."

THE THREE, THE NINE, THE TWELVE, AND THE ONE

These four levels describe the full architecture of The Way:

- **The Three Currents** form the *structure* — the great domains of mastery: Action, Relationship, and Awareness.
- **The Ninefold Virtues** form the *heart* — the living qualities that shape conduct in all things.
- **The Ancestral Twelve** form the *roots* — the older, broader traditions refined into the Nine.

From these layers, The Way expresses its central movement:

The Way flows from the Twelve into the Nine, through the Balance of the Three, and rests in The One.

The One is the practitioner aligned with the Whole — one who lives in harmony with the currents, the virtues, and the greater flow of life.

V. THE ANCESTRAL VIRTUES AND THEIR REFINEMENT INTO THE NINEFOLD CIRCLE

Earlier forms of The Way drew from the classical and chivalric codes of conduct, listing twelve or more virtues. Across traditions, thirteen core traits emerged, later refined into the Ninefold Circle.

Over time, The Way of Still Waters distilled and integrated these overlapping ideas into a cohesive circle of nine — eight living virtues bound by a ninth, the guiding principle of **Balance**.

ORIGINAL VIRTUES (THIRTEEN IN TOTAL AS COMPILED ACROSS SOURCES)

Fair Play • Nobility • Valor • Courtesy • Fidelity • Duty • Integrity • Respect • Courage • Honor • Compassion • Honesty • Loyalty

(Though often referred to as "the Twelve," the historical lists combined elements from several traditions, producing thirteen named traits that naturally clustered into families.)

MERGED LINEAGES

- **Fair Play + Respect → Courtesy** — grace in interaction and fairness in all dealings.

- **Nobility + Fidelity → Honor** — steadfast dignity and loyalty made visible.

- **Valor + Courage → Courage** — the will to act rightly despite fear.

- **Honesty + Integrity → Integrity** — inner wholeness and outward truth.

- **Loyalty + Duty → Duty** — chosen service and faithful responsibility.
- **Compassion** — the open heart that softens strength.
- **Wisdom** — the discerning mind that knows timing and proportion.
- **Humility** — the grounded spirit that tempers pride.

These eight express the living body of The Way. The ninth, **Balance**, is their unifying principle — the still point that governs when to apply each and in what measure.

THE REFINED NINEFOLD CIRCLE

1. **Courage** — Action in the face of fear.
2. **Duty** — Service freely chosen.
3. **Honor** — Integrity expressed outwardly.
4. **Courtesy** — Grace in relationship.
5. **Compassion** — Empathy made motion.
6. **Integrity** — Wholeness between word, thought, and deed.
7. **Wisdom** — Discernment through calm perception.
8. **Humility** — Strength without pride.
9. **Balance** — The harmonizing current that unites them all. Balance is both the ninth virtue and the unseen principle that governs them all — the still axis upon which The Way turns.

VI. THE CODEX Q&A — MORAL ALIGNMENT AND COMPATIBILITY

1. **Is there any justification for cheating on a spouse?**
   No. Betrayal breaks truth and honor. The Way holds fidelity sacred as a form of courage.
2. **Is an online sexual relationship compatible with The Way?**
   Only in honesty. Deception and exploitation break integrity; connection built on truth may still align.
3. **Is ghosting a friend to avoid hard conversations compatible?**
   No. The Way calls for courage in speech and compassion in closure. Avoidance is not peace.
4. **Is vengeance ever justified?**
   Justice, yes; vengeance, no. The first restores Balance — the second feeds chaos.
5. **Can lying ever serve virtue?**
   Only to shield the innocent, never to serve self. Even then, truth must return swiftly.
6. **How should one respond to betrayal?**
   With clarity, not cruelty. Step back, not down; heal the wound without inheriting the poison.
7. **What is right anger?**
   The fire that purifies, not consumes. It burns brightest under control.
8. **What is courage in defeat?**
   To rise again with integrity intact. Failure tests the soul more deeply than success.
9. **How should one treat an enemy?**
   With caution and dignity. The Way judges by conduct, not by opposition.

10. **Can peace coexist with strength?**
    Always. True strength is peace that has learned to stand.
11. **Is mercy weakness?**
    Never. Mercy is compassion wielded with discipline.
12. **How is The Way lived daily?**
    Through reflection, restraint, and renewal: act rightly, flow gracefully, see clearly.

VII. DAILY PRACTICE

Daily practice is the quiet rhythm that keeps the Three Currents—Steel, Water, and Balance—aligned.

These rituals are simple on the surface, yet they shape the entire day's conduct.

They are not ceremonies or obligations, but moments of clarity that return the practitioner to the center of The Way.

Time	Practice	Purpose	Virtues Engaged
Morning Intention	*"Today I will act with virtue and flow with grace."*	Set the tone for the day. Establish a clear stance of strength and compassion before stepping into the world. Morning intention anchors the mind in purpose, ensuring the first steps are taken consciously, not reactively.	Courage, Duty, Integrity
Midday Reset	*"Am I forcing what should be guided?"*	A recalibration point. Midday often brings tension, ego, or fatigue. This question loosens the grip, restores breath, and invites gentleness back into the moment. It shifts the practitioner from strain back into flow.	Temperance, Wisdom, Humility
Evening Reflection	*"Where did I live The Way? Where did I resist it?"*	A practice of honest review—not for guilt, but for growth. Evening reflection clarifies lessons learned, releases the day's emotional residue, and strengthens tomorrow's intention. It returns the waters to stillness before rest.	Honor, Compassion, Integrity

Together, these three moments form a daily cycle of **alignment, adjustment, and refinement**, quietly shaping the practitioner into one who moves with clarity, purpose, and grace.

BOOK II: THE LINEAGE AND LIVING PRACTICE

"THE MOMENT YOU CHOOSE YOURSELF, YOUR LIFE BEGINS TO CHANGE."

PREFACE

The *Way of Still Waters* was born from the meeting of many streams —
the honor of the Samurai, the chivalry of the Knight,
the discipline of the Stoic, the flow of the Taoist,
the courage of the Ranger, the fire of the Klingon,
the calm of the Jedi, the creed of the Mandalorian,
the harmony of the Minbari, the vigilance of the Anla'Shok,
and the compassion of The Doctor, traveler through time and conscience.

Each sought the same eternal truth:
that power and peace are not opposites, but partners —
steel and water — forged together into Balance.

The Way *of Still Waters* is not religion, but practice:
the discipline to act without cruelty,
to feel without drowning,
to walk the line between duty and compassion.

It is **Stillness in Motion** — calm amid the storm, motion without turmoil. Stillness is the state of Balanced awareness — poised between action and surrender.

I. THE LINEAGE OF THE WAY

THE SAMURAI — THE PATH OF RECTITUDE

Rectitude, Courage, Benevolence, Respect, Honesty, Honor, Loyalty.
Discipline and serenity meet in death-awareness:
to act rightly, even when unseen.

THE KNIGHT AND THE RANGER — THE PATH OF GUARDIANSHIP

Chivalry, Courtesy, Fair Play, Fidelity, Nobility.
Serve humbly; protect what cannot protect itself.

THE TAOIST — THE PATH OF FLOW

Wu Wei: effortless action.
Harmony with The Way of all things.
Where Stoicism gives form, Taoism gives breath.

THE STOIC — THE PATH OF REASON

Virtue alone is good.
Accept what you cannot control; master what you can.
Stillness of thought is the first shield.

THE KLINGON — THE PATH OF SONG AND HONOR

Courage without hatred; death accepted as life's verse.
Honor in combat, respect for worthy foes.

THE JEDI — THE PATH OF LIGHT

Serenity, Knowledge, Defense, Balance.

Power only in defense, never domination.
Strength guided by compassion.

THE MINBARI — THE PATH OF UNITY

The three castes — Worker, Warrior, Religious — serve the One.
Strength, craft, and faith in harmony.

THE MANDALORIAN — THE PATH OF CREED

"This is The Way."
Honor through belonging and quiet endurance.
Steel as resilience; water as loyalty.

THE ANLA'SHOK — THE PATH OF SERVICE

"We live for the One, we die for the One."
Vigilance without vanity.
Steel as resolve; water as faith.

THE DOCTOR — THE TRAVELER OF COMPASSION

"Never cruel, never cowardly. Never give up. Never give in."
Compassion through time; mercy in the face of power.
Each regeneration a rebirth through Balance —
ego surrendered, virtue reborn.
The Doctor teaches that cleverness without kindness is chaos,
and courage without mercy is tyranny.
Steel in intellect, water in heart.

"The Klingon sings where The Doctor heals — yet both seek honor in the face of power. One tempers passion with mercy; the other tempers strength with purpose."

II. THE STREAMS OF THE WAY

INTRODUCTION TO THE STREAMS

The Way of Still Waters is not the product of a single culture or philosophy.

It is a river shaped by many tributaries — warrior codes, spiritual teachings, ethical traditions, and modern myths. Each stream offered something essential: a method of discipline, a way of seeing, a model of courage, or an expression of compassion. These influences were not taken whole, but refined and integrated, becoming the foundations upon which The Way stands today.

What follows is a map of those streams and the lessons they contribute to the current of Still Waters. Core lessons are integrated from each source.

- **Stoicism:** Virtue as the highest good; reasoned action; mastery of perception and self; steadiness amid adversity.

- **Taoism:** Harmony through flow; yielding strength; the wisdom of timing; Balance through softness and adaptability.

- **Bushidō (Samurai):** Duty to one's commitments; loyalty and disciplined action; honor lived through consistency; respectful conduct.

- **Chivalry (Knighthood):** Compassion joined with strength; courtesy as a form of dignity; protection of the vulnerable; moral courage.

- **Ranger Ethos:** Guardianship of Balance; silent service;

patient observation; unity with nature and the unseen pathways of life.

- **Jedi Code:** Peace through understanding; mastery of emotion; restraint guided by wisdom; harmony with a greater living force.

- **Klingon Way:** Courage without hatred; bold honesty; honor through decisive action; life embraced as struggle and song; death faced with dignity.

- **Mandalorian Creed:** Discipline and loyalty; identity forged through chosen conduct; devotion to clan and purpose; constancy in one's code.

- **Minbari / Anla'Shok:** "We stand between the candle and the darkness." Service through awareness; unity of mind, spirit, and duty; humble readiness.

- **The Doctor:** Mercy as strength; kindness as courage; refusal of cruelty; virtue proven in extremis—when no reward or witness remains.

Together, these systems form a continuum — each offering a different lesson in how to live with clarity and courage. Their union gives The Way its shape:

Steel to strengthen will,

Water to soften the heart,

Balance to steady the mind.

III. THE STEEL AND WATER MODEL

This model reflects the Three Currents of **Action**, **Relationship**, and **Awareness** in their simplest form. Steel and Water are the two visible forces of The Way; **Balance** is the unseen axis between them — the stillness that allows both to act in harmony. Steel without Water becomes rigid. Water without Steel becomes directionless. Balance unites them into meaningful conduct.

> **"Steel gives form.**
> **Water gives life.**
> **Together they endure."**

Steel — Virtue, Duty, Order, Clarity
Steel represents the structure of the self: disciplined intention, firm choices, and the courage to act rightly. It is the blade of principle — sharp enough to cut through confusion and strong enough to stand against adversity.

Water — Empathy, Adaptability, Peace, Patience
Water is the heart of The Way: compassion made motion, the ability to bend without breaking, and the wisdom to move with circumstances rather than against them. Water softens strength, tempers judgment, and brings gentleness into power.

Balance
Steel is clarity of form; Water is compassion in motion; Balance is their meeting in stillness. It is the quiet center where judgment settles, ego dissolves, and right action becomes clear. Balance prevents Steel from becoming cruelty and Water from becoming surrender.

To master The Way is to become a **living blade** — able to act with strength, yet without cruelty; to move with grace, yet without yielding one's integrity. Steel provides direction, Water provides wisdom, and Balance governs both.

IV. THE THREEFOLD AXIS

The Way rests on three inner dimensions — **Mind, Spirit, and Body** — each drawn from a different ancestral stream, and each essential for a life of Balance.

- **Mind (Stoic): think clearly, act justly.**
  The Mind Axis is disciplined perception: the ability to see the world as it is, not as fear or anger paints it.

  It guides intention, steadies emotion, and ensures that action flows from clarity rather than reaction.

- **Spirit (Taoist): flow with nature, yield with grace.**
  The Spirit Axis is the breath of The Way — the capacity to adapt, soften, and remain aligned with the natural rhythm of events.

  It teaches the practitioner when to move, when to wait, and how to bend without breaking.

- **Body (Warrior): act with duty, serve with strength.**
  The Body Axis is disciplined action: duty carried out with courage, precision, and readiness.

  It grounds virtue in the physical world, turning intention into movement and compassion into service.

Together, these three axes temper one another.

> **Mind without Spirit becomes rigid.**
> **Spirit without Body becomes passive.**
> **Body without Mind becomes reckless.**

Like a blade forged by fire, shaped by hammer, and cooled in water, each element strengthens the others.

When any axis dominates, imBalance weakens the whole.
When all three align, the practitioner stands centered, capable, and whole.

Each axis ultimately returns to **stillness** —
the quiet Balance between action and surrender, effort and ease, Steel and Water.

V. THE NINE WAYS OF STILL WATERS

The Nine Ways are the lived disciplines through which the Nine Virtues are made real. Over time, the Ninefold Virtues gave rise to the Nine Ways — lived expressions that translate principle into daily discipline. Their names may vary, but each flows from its corresponding virtue.

In lived practice, some virtues evolve new names to express their applied form: Fidelity grows from Humility as loyal constancy; Justice arises where Courage and Temperance meet. Thus, every Way remains true to its Virtue. Thus, the Nine Ways are not replacements but reflections — living currents through which the Nine Virtues move in the world.

1. **Integrity — The Way of Clear Reflection**
   Speak no falsehood, even to yourself.
2. **Fidelity — The Way of Steadfast Waters**
   Promises are sacred rivers. Keep them pure.
3. **Courage — The Way of Calm Fire**
   Fear is natural; cowardice is surrender to it.
4. **Compassion — The Way of Gentle Strength**
   Power that heals is divine.
5. **Justice — The Way of the Balanced Sword**
   Strike only to restore harmony. The blade guided by compassion, not pride.
6. **Duty — The Way of the Quiet Path**
   Service done unseen is virtue refined.
7. **Respect — The Way of Upright Bearing**
   Dignity without pride; humility without submission.
8. **Wisdom — The Way of Measured Flow**
   Patience sharpens every blade.

9. **Honor — The Way of Still Waters**
   Peace through Balance; motion through calm.

VI. THE CODEX OF COMPATIBILITY

As the Codex teaches through principle, so must conduct reflect it in action. The Way is not a belief or title — it is a practice. Every choice, spoken or unspoken, public or private, must align with the virtues it claims to serve.

Every act must reflect The Way.

Actions that arise from **cheating, deceit, cowardice, or cruelty** fracture Balance and cloud the inner waters.

Such conduct separates the practitioner from truth, from compassion, and from the clarity required for right action.

Actions grounded in **truth, loyalty, courage, and mercy** restore Balance. They reconnect the practitioner to humility, sincerity, and purpose, renewing the alignment between inner intention and outer deed.

NINE MODERN PRINCIPLES

Modern adaptations of the Nine Virtues

In a world shaped by digital interaction, rapid communication, and constant emotional noise, the ancient virtues take on new expressions. These principles translate the Ninefold Virtues into practical guidance for modern life:

- **Truth in Silence**
  Speak honestly — and stay silent when silence is the kinder truth.

- **Duty in Presence**
  Show up fully; offer your attention as a form of service.

- **Mercy in Judgment**
  Choose compassion over condemnation, especially when you have the power to wound.

- **Loyalty in Absence**
  Honor others when they are not present; speak of them as you would if they stood beside you.

- **Discipline in Emotion**
  Feel fully, but act wisely. Let emotion inform, not control.

- **Honor in Digital Form**
  Conduct online as you would in person — with integrity, respect, and restraint.

- **Grace in Defeat**
  Accept losses with dignity; let humility guide the response to failure or frustration.

- **Stillness in Conflict**
  Hold the center. Do not react from impulse; respond from clarity.

- **Balance in Power**
  Use influence gently. Strength is tested by how it treats the vulnerable.

These principles serve as a bridge between the timeless teachings of the Ninefold Virtues and the complex realities of modern life.

In the modern world, the virtues of The Way adapt to new forms of challenge — digital, social, emotional, and internal.

Yet their essence remains unchanged.

VII. PRACTICE OF THE WAY

The daily practice of The Way brings its teachings from principle into lived experience. The **Circle of Nine** symbolizes the harmony of the virtues in motion, while the **Central Flame** represents the living conscience — the inner light that guides judgment, intention, and action.

Morning Practice:
Choose one Way; live it in deed.

Each day begins with a single chosen virtue or Way, carried intentionally through actions, speech, and small choices. Living one Way deeply is better than touching all nine lightly.

Evening Practice:
"Where was my steel untempered? Where was my water unstill?"

Night returns the practitioner to reflection — not for guilt, but for alignment. These two questions reveal imBalance gently and invite refinement without self-reproach.

Symbol:

The Circle of Nine surrounding the Center Flame — virtue containing conscience, conscience illuminating virtue.

Motto:

Be Steel in Will.
Be Water in Heart.

Oath:

The Oath is the practitioner's vow to carry the Codex into each day, not as an ideal but as a discipline.

I serve peace, not pride.
I wield strength, not for conquest, but for calm.
I stand where chaos meets silence.
My steel is mercy; my water is truth; my stillness is The Way.

This practice forms the living rhythm of The Way — a cycle of intention, action, reflection, and renewal.

AFTERWORD — THE LIVING BLADE

The Way is timeless — a mirror held by many hands.
From Samurai to Knight, from Jedi to Anla'Shok,
each carried stillness into storm.

Peace must sometimes wear armor.
Strength must sometimes kneel.

If you hear the call, you are already one of them.

CLOSING BENEDICTION

When your steel feels heavy, return to water.

When your water feels lost, return to stillness.

When your stillness feels empty, remember

The Way flows through you.

CLOSING MANTRAS

"HOLD VIRTUE; FOLLOW THE CURRENT."

"BE STEEL WHEN DUTY CALLS, WATER WHEN WISDOM WHISPERS."

"HONOR IN THOUGHT. TRUTH IN WORD. COURAGE IN DEED. THUS IS THE CURRENT KEPT CLEAR."

"BE KIND, EVEN WHEN IT COSTS YOU — FOR KINDNESS IS COURAGE REFINED."

"THE ONE WHO CAN CHANGE SHAPE WITHOUT LOSING SELF IS UNBREAKABLE."

"FLOW WITHOUT RIGIDITY; SHAPE THE BANKS RATHER THAN DAMMING THE RIVER."

Thus ends the Codex of Still Waters.
May those who walk it find peace in their motion, and motion in their peace.

"THE ANSWER OFTEN WAITS IN THE QUIET."

BOOK III: LINEAGE OF THE WAY

"EACH CHOICE YOU MAKE SHAPES THE PERSON YOU RISE INTO."

The Way of Still Waters did not emerge from a singular culture, doctrine, or era. It is a *river made of many smaller rivers*, each carrying wisdom shaped by ages of conflict, reflection, philosophy, and story. Some of these influences come from the ancient world. Some arise from myth and legend. And some come from modern fictional traditions that express truths older than civilization itself.

Each tributary provided something essential: a discipline, a virtue, a metaphor, a warning, or a vision of what strength and compassion look like when bound together.

The Way is not a copy of any of these traditions. Rather, it is a synthesis — a deliberate refinement of their best qualities into a living practice of Balance, clarity, dignity, and kindness.

Below are **eleven** streams that converge into The Way, each expanded to give a full and rich understanding of what was taken, why it matters, and how it shapes the Codex.

1. STOICISM — THE DISCIPLINE OF THE INNER WATERS

Stoicism is the backbone of The Way's internal discipline. From Marcus Aurelius, Epictetus, and Seneca, we inherit the idea that while the world is chaotic and beyond control, the self is not. Stoicism teaches that *our judgments shape our suffering,* and that emotional mastery is not suppression, but clarity.

STOICISM TEACHES:

- Virtue is the only true good.
- External events are neutral; perception gives them power.
- Emotions are not enemies, but signals requiring discipline.

- Wisdom comes from distinguishing what is ours to shape.
- Adversity reveals character more than comfort ever will.

From Stoicism, The Way absorbed its doctrine of **inner stillness**, the teaching that turbulent waters distort truth while calm waters reflect it faithfully. The emphasis on *responding rather than reacting* echoes Epictetus. The nightly reflection ritual mirrors Aurelius's Meditations. The belief that strength without virtue is corruption — and that virtue without testing is unproven — runs through the entire Codex.

Stoicism forms the **inner spine** of The Way: a discipline of perception, judgment, and response.

2. TAOISM — THE FLOWING PATH OF BALANCE

Where Stoicism gives structure, Taoism provides breath. The writings of Laozi and Zhuangzi showed that life flows like a river, and suffering comes from resisting the natural movement of things. The Tao is not a rulebook but a harmony to be aligned with.

TAOISM TEACHES:

- Softness overcomes hardness.
- Stillness reveals truth that force conceals.
- Balance is shifting, not static.
- Simplicity is wisdom.
- To lead, one must follow the natural flow.

The Way's core metaphors—*follow the current, shape the banks but do not fight the river,* and *water wears down stone by persistence, not pressure*—come directly from Taoist philosophy.

The fusion of **steel** (form, intent, discipline) and **water** (adaptability, gentleness, patience) is a deliberate Taoist–Bushidō synthesis. From Taoism, The Way gained the spiritual posture of *effortless action*: moving without forcing, acting without grasping, and meeting the world with supple strength.

Taoism forms the **breath and rhythm** of The Way: the art of yielding without surrender.

3. BUSHIDŌ — THE HONOR OF DISCIPLINED ACTION

Bushidō is the pillar of **duty, resolve, and disciplined conduct** within The Way. The samurai traditions of medieval Japan embodied a union of martial readiness and moral responsibility. Their code centered not on violence, but on right action in the face of fear.

BUSHIDŌ TEACHES:

- Integrity without compromise
- Duty held as sacred
- Courtesy as a sign of discipline
- Courage as action in the presence of fear
- Honor as the alignment of inner and outer self

From Bushidō, The Way inherited its solemn respect for promises and the weight carried by one's word. The idea that **character is a blade sharpened by practice** and dulled by inaction deeply informs the Codex.

The symbolic sword in Still Waters is not a weapon, but a metaphor for:

- clarity of purpose
- readiness to act
- the sharp edge of truth
- the disciplined courage to stand firm when required

Bushidō contributes the **discipline of form** to The Way — the steel that complements the softness of water.

Where Bushidō taught duty and discipline, Western chivalry contributed **the heart of protection and compassion.**
Knighthood fused martial power with moral obligation, emphasizing that strength must serve the weak, not dominate them.

CHIVALRY TEACHES:

- Protect the vulnerable
- Serve justice and fairness
- Extend courtesy even to rivals
- Act with courage guided by compassion
- Serve without expectation of reward

From Chivalry, The Way absorbed its strong relational ethic: kindness as strength-in-motion, courtesy as respect embodied, and duty as a joyful act of service.

The knightly tradition also provided the model for **guardianship** — the belief that virtue is not merely inward but expressed through the defense of peace, the shielding of others, and the willingness to stand between harm and the innocent.

Chivalry forms the **heart of compassion** within The Way.

5. RANGER ETHOS — THE QUIET GUARDIAN

The ranger archetype — found in folklore, Tolkien's writings, wilderness guardians, and real-world scouts — introduced the ethic of the **quiet protector**. Rangers do not govern. They guide. They watch. They respond with precision rather than spectacle.

- Observe before acting

- Move quietly, act decisively

- Understand the land and the moment

- Protect those who travel the path

- Strength is found in vigilance, not noise

The Way's concept of the **Watcher by the Water** — the figure who stands unseen at the boundary between calm and chaos — draws heavily from the ranger ideal. Its teachings on awareness, subtlety, and patience come from this lineage. The ranger contributes humility to strength, and wisdom to action.

Ranger ethos forms the **discipline of watchfulness** within The Way.

6. DOCTOR WHO — THE ETHICS OF KINDNESS AND DECENCY

Doctor Who brought to The Way the modern moral pillar of **kindness as strength**. The Doctor stands for courage without cruelty, wisdom without arrogance, and power wielded only in defense of life — never domination.

DOCTOR WHO TEACHES:

- Never be cruel. Never be cowardly.

- Hate is foolish; love is wise.

- Do what is right even when hopeless.

- Kindness is a discipline.

- Actions define morality, not intentions.

The Way absorbed these teachings deeply. Its emphasis on decency, mercy, and self-restraint in the face of anger all derive from the Doctor's example. The Doctor embodies the virtue of

Balance through Compassion — the idea that choosing kindness when hatred is easier is the highest form of courage.

Doctor Who contributes the **moral compass** of The Way. We will take a special look at The Doctor shortly.

7. THE MANDALORIAN CREED — IDENTITY THROUGH CONDUCT

The Mandalorian Creed offers a model of **chosen identity, loyalty, and consistent conduct.** Unlike inherited caste systems, Mandalorian culture emphasizes that one becomes Mandalorian by *choice and discipline* — a principle echoed in The Way.

THE CREED TEACHES:

- Loyalty to clan and chosen family
- Honor demonstrated through action
- Discipline as the foundation of strength
- Protection as duty
- Identity built on conduct, not bloodline

"This is The Way" became more than a catchphrase — it became a philosophical anchor. The Way of Still Waters inherited:

- the concept of a chosen code
- the emphasis on action rather than title
- the belief that identity is forged through practice

We removed Mandalorian harshness and violence, retaining only what aligns with the Codex: **community, loyalty, discipline, and honorable conduct.**

The Creed contributes the **discipline of identity** within The Way.

The Jedi Order contributed **spiritual discipline, emotional mastery, and service-oriented guardianship.** They stand as an archetype for power guided by wisdom, not passion.

THE JEDI TEACH:

- Peace over passion
- Knowledge over ignorance
- Serenity amid conflict
- Harmony with the living Force
- Service without ego

The Way draws from the Jedi a commitment to:

- emotional poise
- acting from clarity, not agitation
- using capability only in defense
- serving a greater good rather than personal ambition

Many parts of the Codex, especially those on emotional maturity, restraint, and non-reactive awareness, trace their lineage to Jedi wisdom.

The Jedi contribute the **discipline of serenity** within The Way.

9. KLINGON HONOR CODE — TRUTH, AUTHENTICITY, COURAGE

Klingon culture, though often depicted as fierce, contains a profound ethic of **honesty, authenticity, and courage**. It provided The Way with a model of truth-speaking and bravery without hatred.

KLINGONS TEACH:

- Speak truth boldly

- Face trials with courage
- Live authentically without shame
- Honor outweighs victory
- Loyalty binds chosen family

The Way adopted Klingon:

- boldness in speech
- courage in adversity
- reverence for truth
- the idea that honor is lived, not claimed

Yet it transformed Klingon aggression into **peaceful moral courage**—courage to confront wrongs, speak truth with dignity, and live authentically.

Klingon ethos contributes the **discipline of truthful courage** to The Way.

10. MINBARI TRADITION — INTEGRATION OF SPIRIT, DISCIPLINE, AND CRAFT

The Minbari offered a model of **harmonious societal structure and spiritual discipline**. Their division into Worker, Warrior, and Religious castes demonstrated that different strengths form a unified whole.

THE MINBARI TEACH:

- Honor across all roles
- Balance between heart, duty, and craft
- Respect for ritual and tradition
- Discipline expressed through purpose
- Seek understanding before conflict

The idea that a complete person integrates **mind, spirit, and action** echoes the Minbari triad. Their reverence for ritual influenced The Way's meditative practices. Their disciplined calm influenced the tone of the Codex. Minbari tradition contributes the **discipline of integrated harmony** within The Way.

11. ANLA'SHOK (RANGERS) — SERVICE WITHOUT GLORY

The Anla'Shok, known simply as the Rangers, represent one of the most essential sources behind The Way of Still Waters. More than any other lineage, they embody the quiet, selfless guardian spirit at the center of the philosophy. Their presence in *Babylon 5* offers a model not of conquest or authority, but of humble watchfulness—protecting life and harmony without seeking recognition or reward.

The Rangers stand for Balance rather than power, service rather than glory, and purpose rather than prestige. They operate on the edges of conflict, preventing harm before it begins, defending those who cannot defend themselves, and accepting that many of their greatest successes will never be known.

Their example resonates deeply with the ethos of Still Waters, where character is defined not by what is proclaimed but by what is practiced in silence.

THE RANGERS TEACH:

- **Live for a higher purpose**
  Service is not about recognition, but alignment with something greater than the self.

- **Die, if needed, for that purpose**
  Courage means accepting risk without letting fear dictate action.

- **Act quietly and humbly**

The most meaningful protections are often unseen and uncelebrated.

- **Train without end**
  Readiness is a form of respect—for those they shield and the mission they uphold.
- **Seek peace, not praise**
  Their work is measured by the safety of others, not by public admiration.

From the Rangers, The Way inherited several defining elements.

First is the principle of **service without glory**.

A practitioner of Still Waters does the right thing whether or not anyone notices. Virtue is not performance; it is lived action carried out with clean intent. The Rangers model a form of courage that avoids spectacle and ego, choosing clarity of purpose over personal recognition.

Second is the value of **quiet readiness**.

Ranger discipline emphasizes training, awareness, and preparation long before a moment of crisis appears. This shaped The Way's understanding that strength is built in everyday habits—through calm practice, steady refinement, and silent mastery. Readiness itself becomes compassion, because it enables protection without hesitation.

Third is the ethic of **acting only when needed**.

The Rangers are decisive, but never reckless. They intervene to restore Balance, not to dominate or impress. This taught The Way the difference between force used with wisdom and force used from pride. Their restraint mirrors the Balance Current: action chosen carefully, guided by clarity rather than impulse.

Fourth is **humility in strength**.

Though highly capable, the Rangers do not boast or seek authority. Their humility is born of purpose, not weakness. This perspective helped shape The Way's belief that true strength does not need to announce itself. Quiet competence is more powerful than loud bravado.

Finally, the Rangers exemplify **purpose over self**.

Their motto—*"We live for the One, we die for the One"*—speaks to alignment with the greater good rather than personal ambition. The Way adapted this into its teaching on The One: the individual who acts in harmony with the greater current of life.

Anla'Shok philosophy ultimately contributed the discipline of **humility, readiness, and purpose** within The Way. It reinforced the idea that the highest work is often unseen, and that the truest guardians are those who stand watch not for praise, but for peace.

CLOSING: THE RIVER MADE WHOLE

These eleven traditions—philosophical, spiritual, ethical, and mythic—merge into one unified current. Stoic clarity, Taoist flow, Samurai resolve, Knightly compassion, Ranger vigilance, the Doctor's kindness, Mandalorian loyalty, Jedi serenity, Klingon courage, Minbari harmony, and Ranger humility all converge to form something new.

The Way of Still Waters is not a copy of any one tradition.
It is a **synthesis** — a river shaped by many streams and made whole by its purpose:
a life lived with Balance, honor, clarity, and compassion.

"NEVER UNDERESTIMATE THE MIRACLE OF BEING YOU."

BOOK IV: THE DOCTOR'S LENS ON THE WAY OF STILL WATERS

"BRAVERY ISN'T THE ABSENCE OF FEAR. IT'S CHOOSING THE DIRECTION ANYWAY."

Drawn from the Teachings of the Wanderer in Time

"Never be cruel. Never be cowardly. Hate is always foolish. Love is always wise. Always try to be nice, but never fail to be kind." — The Doctor

I. ON THE NATURE OF THE WANDERER

Among the many archetypes that walk The Way, there exists one who bears neither sword nor banner, yet stands unyielding against cruelty and despair. This is the Wanderer — the one known to some as The Doctor. They are a knight without armor, a sage without temple, a warrior whose weapon is compassion. Their creed aligns seamlessly with The Way of Still Waters, for it speaks of courage Balanced by mercy, wisdom tempered by love, and steadfastness without violence. To walk in this manner is to embrace the paradox of strength: that true might is measured not in conquest, but in restraint; not in how fiercely one fights, but in how gently one heals.

II. THE CONCORDANCE OF PRINCIPLES

Teaching of the Wanderer	Precept of The Way	Expression in Action
Never be cruel. Never be cowardly.	Courage without cruelty. Valor guided by empathy.	Use force only to protect; never to punish or humiliate.
Hate is always foolish. Love is always wise.	Compassion clarifies; hatred blinds.	Act from love of life, not loathing of foes.
Always try to be nice, but never fail to be kind.	Niceness is courtesy; kindness is sacrifice.	Speak truth with grace, even when it cuts.
I do what I do because it's right — and kind.	Duty rooted in decency.	Serve without expectation of reward or victory.
I'm not trying to win.	Detachment from conquest.	Seek resolution, not triumph. Preserve possibility.
Who I am is where I stand.	Identity through steadfastness.	Hold your ground for the innocent, even when alone.

III. The Protocols of Kindness

- The Offering of the Out: Mercy precedes judgment. Always extend a path toward peace, even to the unworthy.

- The Principle of Least Harm: Choose the gentlest method that fulfills the need. Every life spared honors The Way.

- The Discipline of Truthful Speech: Kindness is not softness. Speak what must be said, but cloak it in compassion.

- The Cleansing of Hatred: Should anger arise, withdraw until stillness returns. Strike no blow from wrath.

- The Duty Before Victory: Let your purpose be protection, not prestige. Triumph means nothing if innocence is lost.

- The Standing of the Threshold: When retreat would condemn others, stand fast. Courage is quiet endurance.

- The Rite of Repair: When the storm has passed, tend the wounded, restore what can be mended, and remember those who fell.

IV. THE EDGE OF THE BLADE — ON THE LAST RESORT

When all mercy has been offered and refused, when delay ensures the suffering of innocents, then — and only then — may the blade be drawn. It shall be wielded without hatred, without vanity, without pleasure. Its purpose is not punishment, but the ending of harm. And when the deed is done, the bearer shall lay down the weapon, and seek atonement through service, reflection, and renewal. So is the Balance preserved.

V. THE CREED OF THE WANDERER

I will not be cruel; I will not be cowardly.
I will purge hatred and act with wise love.

I will choose kindness, even when it costs.
I will protect before I prevail, and repair after I act.
Who I am is where I stand — beside the frightened — until the storm breaks.

VI. REFLECTION

The Doctor teaches that kindness is not weakness, that gentleness is not surrender, and that standing unarmed before cruelty is the highest form of bravery. Thus The Way of Still Waters embraces this teaching: to guard without hate, to fight without malice, and to love without condition — even unto the end of one's days.

VII. THE DOCTOR'S TEACHINGS — THE KINDNESS OF POWER

From the wisdom of *The Doctor* comes a living mirror of The Way:

"Never be cruel. Never be cowardly. Hate is always foolish. Love is always wise. Always try to be nice, but never fail to be kind."

The Doctor's creed turns compassion into commandment — a discipline of mercy, not weakness. He stands as a master of **Balance through Compassion**, proving that the greatest strength is self-restraint guided by love. Each teaches that strength without compassion is tyranny, and compassion without strength is surrender. Between them lies The Way.

VIII. THE DOCTRINE OF VIRTUE IN EXTREMIS

"Goodness is not goodness that seeks advantage.
Good is good in the final hour, in the deepest pit,
without hope, without witness, without reward.
Virtue is only virtue in extremis."

These words distill the essence of The Way: True virtue does not depend on comfort, approval, or outcome. It remains when all reward is gone, when no one sees, when hope itself has vanished.

To act rightly *then* — when every lesser reason has burned away — is to live The Way in its purest form.

IX. LESSONS CARRIED INTO THE WAY

From *The Doctor*, The Way learns:

- **Kindness is not softness** — it is courage refined by empathy.
- **Mercy is not surrender** — it is mastery of anger.
- **Hope is not ignorance** — it is the refusal to let darkness dictate conduct.
- **Virtue is proven only in extremis** — when the world offers no reason but the right itself.

To live by this creed is to choose light without guarantee, to hold the current of goodness even in the storm.

"I do what I do because it's right — because it's decent — and above all, it's kind."

Thus The Doctor becomes the compassionate embodiment of Still Waters — a traveler who stands unarmed yet unbroken, who faces cruelty with conscience, and who reminds all who walk The Way that **the truest power is the will to be kind when it would be easier to hate.**

BOOK V: RELATIONAL ETHICS AND ALTERNATIVE RELATIONSHIP STRUCTURES

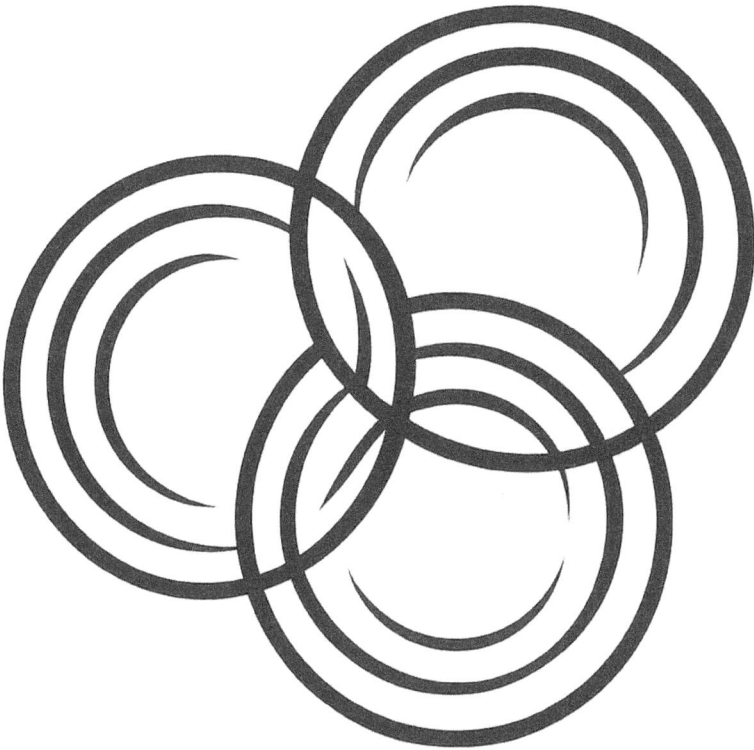

"HEALTHY LOVE DOES NOT PULL YOU OFF YOUR PATH. IT WALKS BESIDE YOU."

The Way does not prescribe monogamy or non-monogamy. It prescribes **conduct** — truth, honor, compassion, responsibility, Balance, and non-harm. Any relational structure may align with The Way if practiced with integrity.

PURPOSE OF THIS BOOK

Within The Way of Still Waters, relationships are not defined by structure, labels, or tradition. They are defined by **conduct**, **alignment**, and the **impact** they leave upon the hearts involved.

This chapter exists to guide practitioners of The Way in all relational forms — romantic, platonic, familial, sexual, communal, and spiritual — so they may act with honor, clarity, Balance, and compassion in every human bond.

The goal is not to dictate who or how one may love. The goal is to illuminate *how to love responsibly*, in alignment with the virtues and principles of The Way.

This chapter provides:

- A universal ethical foundation for all relationships.
- Guidance for navigating modern relational structures.
- Conduct principles for honesty, consent, communication, and boundaries.
- Tools for recognizing when a relationship supports or erodes one's alignment.
- Practices for navigating conflict, healing, repair, and endings with honor.

The Way teaches that our relational conduct reflects our inner stillness or our inner turbulence. It is the mirror in which we see our true discipline.

This chapter covers:

1. **Universal Principles of Relational Ethics**

Foundational guidelines that apply to *every* relationship, regardless of type.

2. **Virtue-Based Relational Pillars**

How Truth, Honor, Compassion, Consent, Responsibility, Balance, and Non-Harm express themselves in human connection.

3. **Relationship Structures and Their Alignment**

A detailed examination of:

- Monogamy and committed partnership
- Ethical non-monogamy
- Polyamory
- Swinging and recreational intimacy
- Friends with benefits and casual connection
- The distinction between ethical openness and cheating
- Emotional affairs and attachment boundaries

This section does not promote or forbid any structure; it defines the conduct necessary for each to remain in harmony with The Way.

4. **Tools for Conduct and Communication**

Including:

- Boundary expression
- Accountability and repair

- Navigating conflict without cruelty
- Recognizing and ending misaligned relationships
- Returning to internal Balance
- The Sixfold Alignment Test for relational clarity

5. **Closing Doctrine**

A unifying philosophical statement summarizing relational ethics in The Way.

CORE STATEMENT

"The Way does not command the form your relationships must take. The Way commands the integrity with which you walk them."

THE FOUNDATIONAL RELATIONAL PILLARS

These seven pillars define the virtues required for all relationships — romantic, platonic, familial, sexual, and communal — to remain aligned with The Way of Still Waters. They are not rules, but **orientations of the heart**, guiding one's conduct toward clarity, dignity, compassion, and Balance.

Each pillar below includes:

- **Doctrine** — the ideal
- **Practice** — how it manifests in real relationships
- **Misalignment** — what violates the principle

---

1. TRUTH

Doctrine of Honesty, Clarity, and Compassionate Integrity

Truth is the foundation of all honorable connection. Without truth, no consent is real, no love is steady, and no bond can endure the tides of life.

Truth must be **clear**, **clean**, and **kind** — honest in substance, compassionate in delivery. Truth that harms by distortion is deceit; truth that harms by cruelty is brutality.

The Way requires neither. The Way requires both honesty and humanity.

To live Truth in relational conduct means:

Speak clearly

- Communicate without deception, distortion, or strategic vagueness
- Align words and actions so they form a single reality

Reveal what others need to choose freely

- Share the information required for informed consent
- Hold no secret worlds that would wound another if revealed

Name your inner world honestly

- Speak feelings, intentions, and concerns plainly
- Share truth **early**, before harm grows or mistrust forms

Deliver truth without cruelty

- Speak with clarity, not venom
- Correct without punishing
- Guide without using truth as a blade

Truth should illuminate — not scorch.

Truth is violated by:

- Lies of commission or omission

- Half-truths used to shape or manipulate outcomes
- Withholding information that directly affects another's well-being
- Acting with hidden agendas or "playing innocent"
- Presenting different versions of yourself to avoid accountability
- Speaking truth with the intent to injure, humiliate, or dominate

When truth is bent, the bond is bent with it. When truth is weaponized, the bond is wounded by the hand that wields it.

CORE PRINCIPLE

Truth must be whole enough to trust, and gentle enough to hear.

This is the Balance of The Way.

---

2. HONOR

Doctrine of Sovereignty, Dignity, and Boundaried Respect

Honor is the recognition that every person is a sovereign being — not an object to be used, controlled, or shaped for convenience.

To honor another is to treat their heart, their choices, and their boundaries as sacred. To honor yourself is to maintain integrity, dignity, and the limits required for your well-being.

Honor requires strength without domination, and boundaries without aggression. It asks: **"Do I leave this person more whole than I found them?"**

To live Honor in relationships means:

Respect Sovereignty

- Acknowledge the autonomy, agency, and right of others to choose freely
- Reject manipulation, coercion, guilt, or emotional pressure
- Treat every heart as sacred, never disposable

Align Conduct With Integrity

- Be dependable, consistent, and trustworthy
- Match actions to promises; match promises to capacity
- Uphold agreements or acknowledge and repair when you cannot

Hold Boundaries With Balance

- State boundaries clearly, without concealment or edge
- Uphold them consistently, without aggression or hostility
- Treat boundaries as expressions of self-respect — never as threats, demands, or ultimatums
- Recognize that a boundary defines **your** limits, not another's obedience

Preserve Dignity — Yours and Theirs

- Choose behaviors that uplift rather than diminish
- Maintain respect even in conflict
- Decline to treat people as replaceable, lesser, or as tools for validation

Honor is the quiet strength that protects connection without controlling it.

Honor is broken when:

- Manipulation replaces clarity
- Coercion replaces consent
- Guilt replaces communication
- Agreements are violated without acknowledgement or repair
- Intimacy is used as leverage or currency
- People are treated as interchangeable or unworthy of respect
- Boundaries are weaponized or ignored

Dishonor fractures not only the bond, but also the self.

Honor sustains dignity — for yourself, for others, and for the bond between you.

This is the Balance of The Way.

---

3. CONSENT

Doctrine of Sovereignty, Safety, and Freedom of Choice

Consent is the right of every soul to choose what happens to their mind, body, heart, and time. It is the foundation of mutual respect, healthy connection, and aligned relationship.

Consent must be **free**, **informed**, **enthusiastic**, and **ongoing** —

never assumed, coerced, or extracted through fear, silence, or obligation.

Consent is sacred. Without it, nothing is aligned with The Way.

PRACTICE

To live Consent in relational conduct means:

Ensure consent is freely given

- Choices must arise without pressure, fear, or emotional leverage
- No guilt, insecurity, or consequences may be used to influence decisions
- Silence is not agreement; hesitation is not consent; endurance is not willingness

Provide clarity and truthful information

- Consent requires honesty, transparency, and mutual understanding
- False information, omission, or distortion invalidates any consent given
- Expectations, roles, and intentions must be openly defined and revisited

Honor boundaries and ongoing choice

- Consent must remain active, not a one-time contract
- Feelings change; circumstances evolve — therefore consent must be revisited
- A withdrawal of consent must be respected immediately, even when inconvenient

Maintain emotional safety

- Never withhold affection to force compliance
- Never weaponize silence
- Never create consequences for honesty
- Never use fear, guilt, or attachment to engineer compliance

Aligned consent is a space where every person's "yes" is real — not coerced, not assumed, not extracted.

MISALIGNMENT

Consent is violated through:

- Pressure disguised as persuasion
- "Going along with it" due to fear of loss or conflict
- Presenting false or incomplete information to obtain agreement
- Ignoring discomfort, hesitation, or withdrawal
- Assuming access without reconfirming
- Using guilt, silence, or affection as tools of control

Any consent gained through fear, manipulation, distortion, or obligation is not consent at all.

CORE PRINCIPLE

Consent requires freedom, clarity, honesty, and emotional safety. Without these, the bond is not mutual — it is coercive.

This is the Balance of The Way.

---

4. COMPASSION

Doctrine of Empathy, Care, and Unpossessive Love

Compassion is the willingness to hold another's experience as real, valid, and worthy of care — even when it differs from your own.

It is the practice of responding to another's humanity with gentleness rather than control, understanding rather than judgment, and presence rather than possession.

Compassion does not cage, correct, or claim. It honors the truth that love is connection, not containment.

To love with compassion is to invite, not demand; to welcome, not grasp; to support, not suffocate.

Compassion strengthens all bonds. Its absence fractures them.

PRACTICE

To live Compassion in relational conduct means:

Care for emotional reality

- Listen to understand, not to defend
- Acknowledge feelings without dismissing or diminishing them
- Offer comfort, patience, and presence when needed
- Consider the emotional impact of your choices

Speak truth gently

- Share truth in ways that do not deliberately wound
- Be kind in conflict, not cruel
- Communicate with clarity but without sharpness or contempt

Love without possessing

- Respect individuality, even in deep partnership

- Recognize that love grants connection — not ownership
- Avoid clinging, controlling, or shaping another's path
- Allow love to remain steady, open, and unforced

Offer compassion even in difference

- You need not share an experience to care about it
- Honor another's vulnerability instead of mocking it
- Treat their inner world as legitimate, even when unfamiliar to you

Compassion is active, not passive; it is the expression of care through conduct, not merely sentiment.

MISALIGNMENT

Compassion is abandoned through:

- Mocking vulnerability
- Using someone's feelings against them
- Being intentionally harsh or unkind in conflict
- Belittling or dismissing emotions
- Showing indifference to suffering, especially suffering you caused
- Treating love as possession, entitlement, or control
- Caging, clinging, or dictating another's choices under the guise of affection

Where compassion is absent, harm begins.

CORE PRINCIPLE

Compassion is kindness in truth, gentleness in conflict, and love without possession.

It is the soft strength that protects connection without controlling it.

This is the Balance of The Way.

---

5. RESPONSIBILITY

Doctrine of Accountability, Integrity, and Self-Respect

Responsibility is the practice of owning the effects of your choices — not merely the intentions behind them. It is the anchor that keeps conduct aligned, relationships steady, and the self grounded in dignity.

Responsibility requires accountability for harm, stewardship of one's inner world, and the courage to maintain self-respect even in connection. To abandon responsibility is to abandon the integrity that holds all bonds together.

PRACTICE

To live Responsibility in relational conduct means:

Own your actions fully

- Take accountability without deflection, blame, or justification
- Repair harm where repair is possible, and acknowledge it where it is not
- Treat mistakes as errors to correct — not rights to repeat

Steward your inner landscape

- Manage your own insecurities, jealousy, and triggers
- Do not expect others to handle your emotional storms

- Regulate yourself rather than displacing your turmoil onto the relationship

Communicate needs responsibly

- Speak your needs clearly rather than hoping others can read them
- Bring concerns forward early, before resentment forms
- Be reliable in both word and deed — consistency is a form of care

Honor your own dignity

- Never shrink yourself to maintain a connection
- Do not silence your needs, minimize your worth, or tolerate mistreatment
- Refuse to accept crumbs as if they were abundance
- Maintain boundaries that preserve your self-respect, even if the connection is lost

Connection that requires self-erasure is not connection at all. Responsibility means choosing actions that honor both the bond and the self.

MISALIGNMENT

Responsibility is forsaken through:

- Blaming others for your behaviors
- Making excuses instead of making amends
- Ghosting, withdrawing, or disappearing to avoid consequences
- Expecting others to fix or manage your internal struggles
- Allowing connection to override dignity

- Silencing yourself to maintain peace
- Accepting mistreatment as the price of belonging

Irresponsibility fractures trust in others — and fractures the self from within.

CORE PRINCIPLE

Responsibility is the courage to face your impact, repair what you can, and refuse to abandon your own dignity.

This is the Balance of The Way.

---

6. BALANCE

Doctrine of Equilibrium, Alignment, and Self-Preserving Connection

Balance is the art of holding connection without losing yourself and holding yourself without abandoning connection.

It is the steady center between extremes — not too tight, not too distant; not self-erasure, not isolation.

Balance allows love to flow cleanly, without chaos, control, or collapse.

A Balanced heart sees clearly, chooses wisely, and loves without sacrificing its own stability.

PRACTICE

To live Balance in relational conduct means:

Hold boundaries that protect connection

- Maintain healthy, consistent limits
- Know when to lean in and when to step back

- Stay grounded in your values even during relational storms

Avoid extremes

- Do not cling or withdraw without awareness
- Do not over-give or under-give
- Do not use control, obsession, avoidance, or neglect as strategies
- Keep your identity and integrity intact within connection

Choose nourishing relationships

- Seek connections that strengthen rather than deplete
- Honor the need for solitude, reflection, and self-regulation
- Keep your inner peace steady instead of chasing validation or escaping discomfort

Leave patterns that harm

- A single wound may be accidental; a pattern reveals a truth the other person is choosing
- Do not stay in spaces where your peace, worth, or stability are consistently eroded
- Departing misalignment is not failure — it is a return to The Way
- The path away from repeated harm is a path toward Balance, not away from love

Balance is not passivity; it is deliberate regulation of your presence, energy, and direction.

MISALIGNMENT

Balance is lost through:

- Emotional clinginess or emotional withdrawal
- Sacrificing identity or integrity to keep someone
- Over-investing or under-investing
- Confusing chaos with passion or intimacy
- Using relationships to avoid solitude or self-examination
- Enduring repeated harm under the guise of loyalty or love

Imbalance distorts perception, weakens connection, and pulls you away from yourself.

CORE PRINCIPLE

Balance is the steady middle path — The Way of aligned connection, self-respect, and the courage to leave what continually harms.

This is the Balance of The Way.

---

7. NO HARM

Doctrine of Gentleness, Integrity, and Non-Destructive Conduct

No Harm is the commitment to avoid causing unnecessary pain — to others or to oneself.

It is the discipline of moving through relationships without cruelty, domination, or self-betrayal.

To walk The Way is to walk gently, even when firmness is required.

No Harm does not mean avoiding conflict; it means conducting conflict with respect. It does not mean avoiding endings; it means honoring endings with the same grace as beginnings. It does not mean staying silent; it means speaking truth that heals rather than cuts.

No Harm is the quiet strength that keeps connection aligned and the self intact.

PRACTICE

To live No Harm in relational conduct means:

1. **Protect dignity — yours and theirs**

   - Refuse to remain where your worth is steadily eroded
   - End connections that cause repeated harm or diminish your spirit
   - Do not betray yourself to keep another
   - Honor your own truth, needs, and well-being as part of relational integrity

2. **Conduct conflict with respect, not domination**

   - Name the issue, not attack the person
   - Stay curious rather than defensive
   - Listen to understand, not to win
   - Disagree without degrading

Domination has no place in The Way. If someone must lose for you to feel whole, you have already left the path.

3. **Speak truth gently**

   - Use honesty to guide, illuminate, and repair

- Avoid using truth as a blade to punish, shame, or overpower
- Communicate with clarity and steadiness, not cruelty or contempt

4. **Honor change as part of alignment**

- Recognize that consent, desires, and capacities evolve
- Accept change with grace rather than punishment
- Adjust agreements openly when the heart shifts

You must allow others the same freedom you seek for yourself.

5. **Honor endings with the dignity of beginnings**

- Offer clarity instead of avoidance
- Express gratitude rather than bitterness
- Use truth rather than excuses
- Seek closure instead of lingering ambiguity

A relationship may end — honor should not.

6. **Leave a gentle wake**

- Every word, action, and silence leaves a trail behind it.
- Ask yourself: *"Does my presence bring steadiness or confusion? Calm or chaos?"*
- Aligned conduct leaves others more whole, not more wounded.

7. **Do not use love or connection as tools of harm**

- Do not wound others to rebalance your ego
- Do not stay in dynamics that corrode self-worth

- Do not tolerate what consistently diminishes your inner steadiness
- Do not mix chaos with intimacy or use relationships as escapes from healing

8. **Let connection serve growth, not stagnation**

Aligned relationships:

- Uplift
- Nourish
- Refine character
- Support healing rather than replace it

A bond that feeds insecurity, chaos, or regression stands outside The Way.

9. **Seek more than safety**

- Safety is the minimum, not the goal.
- The Way calls for relationships that uplift, enrich, and support emotional steadiness.
- Connection should expand the heart, not merely avoid harm.

MISALIGNMENT

Harm occurs when:

- You tolerate what steadily diminishes your spirit
- You intentionally wound others for power, control, or ego
- You stay in patterns that corrode worth or peace
- You use truth as a weapon rather than a guide
- You replace curiosity with domination in conflict

- You punish others for changing or growing
- You end relationships with cruelty, avoidance, or ambiguity
- You betray yourself to keep a connection
- You leave chaos in your wake

Where harm is present, alignment dissolves.

CORE PRINCIPLE

No Harm is the vow to move through relationships with gentleness, clarity, and respect — maintaining dignity, protecting peace, and refusing patterns that wound.

This is the Balance of The Way.

MONOGAMY AND ETHICAL VOWS

Monogamy, within The Way of Still Waters, is not defined by exclusivity alone. It is defined by the **quality of commitment**, the **clarity of agreements**, and the **honor with which one upholds both**.

Monogamy is a sacred vow only when chosen freely, practiced consciously, and maintained with truth, compassion, Balance, and responsibility. It is not superior to other relational forms — but it carries its own unique ethical demands.

Below is its full Codex treatment.

1. THE ESSENCE OF MONOGAMY IN THE WAY

Doctrine

Monogamy is a chosen path of exclusive romantic and sexual connection between two partners. Its ethical power comes not from the exclusivity itself, but from the **honor** with which that exclusivity is upheld.

True monogamy is:

- freely chosen
- actively maintained
- rooted in mutual respect
- adaptable through honest communication

It is not the presence of "only one partner," but the presence of **only one truth**, shared and upheld by both.

---

2. WHEN MONOGAMY IS ALIGNED WITH THE WAY

Monogamy is fully compatible with The Way when it is:

Freely Chosen

Not assumed, inherited, pressured, or demanded. It must be a conscious agreement between equals.

Mutually Understood

Both partners agree on:

- what exclusivity means
- what boundaries exist
- what counts as betrayal
- what transparency is required

Unspoken expectations breed dishonor.

Practiced With Honor

Meaning you:

- uphold promises without secret exceptions
- communicate discomfort before it becomes resentment
- protect the bond proactively
- treat the relationship as a living commitment, not a static default

Supported by Truth and Openness

Healthy monogamy requires:

- honest conversations about desire
- transparency about temptations

- willingness to navigate challenges together

Rooted in Growth, Not Ownership

Monogamy must not be used to control, limit, or possess the other. Exclusive relationship ≠ ownership of a person.

Sustained Through Responsibility

Both partners must contribute to:

- emotional maintenance
- conflict resolution
- continued intimacy
- tending to the bond

Monogamy fails when treated as "set it and forget it."

---

3. WHEN MONOGAMY IS NOT ALIGNED WITH THE WAY

Monogamy becomes misaligned when it is:

Used as Ownership

When one partner treats exclusivity as a claim over time, body, or freedom.

Used as Avoidance

When monogamy is chosen simply to avoid jealousy, vulnerability, or complexity — rather than from true desire.

Assumed By Default

Beginning a relationship without discussing expectations and simply presuming monogamy is a form of unspoken coercion.

Enforced Through Threats or Guilt

If someone stays monogamous only because they fear punishment, loss, abandonment, or shame, consent is not truly present.

Maintained Through Self-Betrayal

If one partner must abandon their true needs, identity, or happiness to keep the monogamous bond intact, the relationship has already drifted outside The Way.

Broken by Lies

A monogamous bond without truth is monogamy only in name, not in practice.

––––––––––

4. ETHICAL DEMANDS UNIQUE TO MONOGAMY

While all relationship structures require truth, monogamy places special weight on:

Exclusive Vulnerability

There is only one partner to turn to for:

- emotional intimacy
- sexual connection
- primary support

This is a gift, and a responsibility.

Transparency of Heart

Since emotional and sexual intimacy are exclusive, partners must share evolving truths about:

- desires
- fears
- needs

- evolving boundaries

Silence erodes monogamy faster than conflict.

Managing Attraction Ethically

Attraction outside the relationship is natural. Acting on it is a choice.

Aligned partners:

- acknowledge attractions without shame
- communicate when temptation threatens stability
- address relational weaknesses that make wandering appealing

Suppressing these truths leads to betrayal; sharing them leads to growth.

Protecting the Bond Proactively

This includes:

- nurturing connection
- maintaining friendship and intimacy
- addressing resentment early
- creating shared rituals of closeness

Monogamy collapses not from single moments, but from neglected seasons.

———

5. THE HONOR OF THE VOW

In The Way, the monogamous promise is considered sacred only when:

- spoken honestly

- upheld consistently
- revisited periodically
- maintained by both partners equally

A vow is not static. It must be re-chosen through action.

When a monogamous bond is healthy, it becomes:

- a sanctuary for the heart
- a crucible for growth
- a steadying force in turbulent times
- a source of deep mutual expansion

Monogamy, at its best, produces a calm so profound that both partners grow into better versions of themselves.

---

6. FIVE MONOGAMY-SPECIFIC QUESTIONS OF THE WAY

Q1: How do we maintain desire in long-term monogamy?

By treating intimacy as a relationship within the relationship — tended, refreshed, and openly discussed.

Q2: What if one partner's needs change?

Needs evolve. Agreements must evolve with them. Refusing to revisit boundaries is a silent form of betrayal.

Q3: Is fantasizing about others misaligned?

No — fantasy is natural. Secrecy and shame are the dangers, not imagination.

Q4: What if one partner wants monogamy and the other does not?

This is a values conflict, not a negotiation. Neither should be coerced; both truths must be honored.

Q5: When does monogamy become harmful?

When it demands self-erasure, isolation, or emotional starvation; when it forbids truth; when it persists only because one fears being alone.

---

7. CORE DOCTRINE OF MONOGAMY IN THE WAY

"Monogamy is honorable not because it is exclusive, but because it is kept in truth."

"The Way does not sanctify possession. It sanctifies chosen devotion."

"A monogamous bond must be re-chosen, re-tended, and re-honored — or it ceases to be monogamy at all."

NON-MONOGAMY AND OTHER STRUCTURES

ETHICAL NON-MONOGAMY & POLYAMORY

SWINGING & RECREATIONAL INTIMACY

FRIENDS WITH BENEFITS & CASUAL CONNECTION

CHEATING, BETRAYAL & THE PATH BACK TO HONOR

EMOTIONAL AFFAIRS & ATTACHMENT BOUNDARIES

Are polyamory, swinging, and friends-with-benefits compatible with The Way?

Short answer:
They *can* be compatible — but only if they follow all pillars of The Way, *especially* Honor, Truth, Consent, Compassion, Responsibility, and No Harm.

Long answer:
Each relational style must be evaluated by *how it is practiced*, not by the label.

The Way is not prescriptive about monogamy vs. non-monogamy — it is prescriptive about **conduct**, **alignment**, and **impact**.

The full breakdowns follow.

ETHICAL NON-MONOGAMY AND POLYAMORY

Ethical Non-Monogamy (ENM) and Polyamory within The Way of Still Waters emphasize *integrity of conduct*, not quantity of partners.

Where monogamy centers on exclusive devotion, ENM centers on **honest plurality**, **responsible transparency**, and **compassionate management of complexity**.

The Way does not treat ENM as inferior, superior, or alternative — only different, and requiring its own form of discipline.

Below is the full expansion.

---

1. THE ESSENCE OF ETHICAL NON-MONOGAMY

Doctrine

Ethical Non-Monogamy is the intentional maintenance of multiple romantic and/or sexual connections, practiced with truth, consent, honor, compassion, responsibility, and Balance.

Unlike betrayal, which hides, ENM reveals. Its ethics hinge on **shared knowledge**, not secrecy.

ENM is aligned with The Way when:

- it is chosen consciously
- it prioritizes emotional responsibility
- it honors boundaries of all partners

- it avoids harm through truth and clarity

It is not "freedom without consequence." It is **commitment to many truths**, navigated with care.

---

2. POLYAMORY DEFINED IN THE WAY

Polyamory is the practice of cultivating *multiple romantic connections* with the full knowledge and consent of all involved.

Polyamory is not:

- a workaround for monogamy
- a justification for cheating
- emotional exploitation
- collecting partners
- evading intimacy by dispersing it

Polyamory is:

- multiple loves carried with full responsibility
- emotional honesty with all parts of the heart
- managing time, care, and truth with maturity
- honoring each connection as its own living bond

Within The Way, polyamory is a deliberate path — one requiring advanced relational skill.

---

3. REQUIREMENTS FOR ENM AND POLYAMORY TO REMAIN IN ALIGNMENT

RADICAL TRUTHFULNESS

More partners require more truth, not less. ENM fails when truths are staggered, softened, or selectively hidden.

Aligned truth includes:

- declaring existing partners before new connections
- discussing the depth and nature of each bond
- naming expectations clearly
- revealing potential conflicts or insecurities

Silence is deception in ENM.

INFORMED, ENTHUSIASTIC CONSENT

Every partner must know:

- the structure
- who else is involved
- the agreed boundaries
- their role and place

Consent cannot be coerced, guilted, or quietly assumed.

EMOTIONAL RESPONSIBILITY

Practitioners must:

- manage their own jealousy
- recognize patterns of attachment
- tend to all partners without neglect
- communicate needs openly
- avoid creating relational hierarchies by default

Polyamory without emotional responsibility is merely chaos with a philosophy.

COMPASSIONATE TIMING

Adding new partners or deepening bonds requires:

- sensitivity to other partners' stability
- gradual integration
- awareness of emotional capacity and bandwidth

Rushing growth fractures foundations.

BOUNDARIES HELD WITH HONOR

Each partner has unique boundaries, including:

- sexual safety
- scheduling
- emotional transparency
- vetoes in some structures
- communication frequency

Boundaries must be agreed upon and upheld — not bent opportunistically.

BALANCING MANY HEARTS WITHOUT LOSING YOUR OWN

The practitioner must monitor:

- their own energy
- their own needs
- their own capacity

If tending multiple bonds erodes personal stability or any partner's peace, alignment must be reevaluated.

---

4. WHERE ENM & POLYAMORY BECOME MISALIGNED WITH THE WAY

ENM fails when it becomes:

- a shield against commitment

- a justification to act without accountability
- emotional consumption disguised as openness
- a way to fill voids rather than grow connections
- a distraction from unresolved trauma
- a tool to avoid loneliness
- a playground for ego
- an escape from honesty

Misalignment typically appears when:

- one partner is coerced
- one partner is ignored
- agreements are broken
- discomfort is minimized
- structure becomes an excuse for inconsistency

The Way requires that each heart involved must be honored as deeply as the primary self.

---

5. THE FIVE POLYAMOROUS STRUCTURES, AND THEIR ALIGNMENT

1. **Hierarchical Polyamory (Primary/Secondary Models)**

Aligned when:

- hierarchies are explicit
- roles are clearly defined
- expectations are shared

Misaligned when:

- hierarchy is hidden

- "secondary" becomes "lesser"
- promises are used as leverage

2. Non-Hierarchical (Egalitarian) Polyamory

Aligned when:

- all partners know the structure
- emotional bandwidth supports equal investment

Misaligned when:

- egalitarianism is declared but not practiced
- time, energy, or priority consistently contradicts stated equality

3. Solo Polyamory

Aligned when:

- autonomy is clear
- partners understand the soloist's independence

Misaligned when:

- "solo" becomes a shield from responsibility
- partners are denied clarity about their significance

4. Kitchen-Table Polyamory

Aligned when:

- all partners consent to interconnectedness
- communication remains transparent

Misaligned when:

- pressure is applied for all partners to be close
- discomfort is pathologized rather than respected

5. **Parallel Polyamory**

Aligned when:

- partners understand their separateness
- lines of privacy are clear but not deceptive

Misaligned when:

- "privacy" becomes secrecy
- partners are deliberately isolated from truths they need

---

6. POLYAMORY-SPECIFIC ETHICAL MANDATES IN THE WAY

Mandate 1: No Shadows

Nothing that affects another partner's well-being may be hidden from them.

Mandate 2: No Substitutions

New love does not replace old love; it must not starve one bond to feed another.

Mandate 3: No Emotional Exploitation

Do not take more affection, intimacy, or attention than you can responsibly return.

Mandate 4: No Forced Enlightenment

Polyamory must not be imposed under the guise of "expanded thinking" or "higher love."

Mandate 5: No Sacrifice of Self or Others

Do not break yourself to meet everyone's needs; Do not let others break themselves to meet yours.

---

7. FIVE ETHICAL QUESTIONS OF POLYAMORY IN THE WAY

Q1: How do I know if polyamory is right for me?

If tending multiple hearts deepens your integrity, joy, and discipline — not your emptiness.

Q2: What if one partner begins to struggle with jealousy?

You slow down, tend to the wound, reinforce safety, and navigate the fear together — not dismiss it.

Q3: What if a new relationship destabilizes an existing one?

You stabilize the original bond before expanding further. New love must not be built on the ruins of neglected foundations.

Q4: Can polyamory exist without hierarchy?

Yes — but only when emotional capacity and time allow for actual equality, not aspirational equality.

Q5: What if I fall in love more deeply with one partner?

Depth is allowed; betrayal is not. Shifting dynamics require truth, negotiation, and re-alignment — not secret re-prioritization.

---

8. CORE DOCTRINE OF ETHICAL NON-MONOGAMY IN THE WAY

"Ethical Non-Monogamy is not freedom from commitment. It is commitment to many truths."

"Polyamory is not the multiplication of desire; it is the multiplication of responsibility."

"**Where monogamy requires depth with one, polyamory requires depth with clarity for all.**"

"**Love may multiply, but honor must never divide.**"

POLYAMORY

Compatible if:

- All partners know about each other — *no secrecy, no half-truths, no triangulation.*
- Consent is enthusiastic, informed, and ongoing.
- Emotional responsibility is practiced (not using new partners to escape problems with existing ones).
- Boundary keeping is clear and honored.
- There is no spiritual or emotional exploitation.
- Compassion and care are distributed honorably, not as a means of manipulation.

Incompatible if:

- It is used as a loophole to cheat.
- One partner is pressured into "agreeing" because they fear losing the relationship.
- It erodes self-respect, peace, or stability.
- Partners are treated as disposable or interchangeable.

The Way's Verdict:

Polyamory *can* align with The Way, but only when practiced with excellent truth, duty, compassion, and clarity.

————————

Q1: *How do I know if I'm truly choosing polyamory, and not just afraid of committing?*

A: The Way asks you to examine your **root motive**.

- If polyamory feels like a way to avoid vulnerability, depth, or being fully seen, it leans out of alignment.

- If it arises from a genuine capacity to love multiple people with **responsibility**, **consistency**, and **care**, it can align with The Way.

The heart check: "Am I expanding my capacity to love responsibly, or escaping the weight of real commitment?"

If it's escape, it's not The Way.

Q2: *What if one partner is naturally monogamous and the other is polyamorous?*

A: This is a **deep values difference**, not just a preference. The Way requires:

- Clear naming of the mismatch.

- No coercion, no "wearing down" the monogamous partner.

- Honesty about whether each person can live this reality without resentment or self-erasure.

If one person has to **shrink their truth** to keep the other, the arrangement is not in harmony with The Way. The Way honors both truths, even if that leads to a parting.

Q3: *How do I practice jealousy management in polyamory according to The Way?*

A: The Way does not demand you be free of jealousy; it asks you to be **honest and responsible** with it.

- Name jealousy without blame: "I feel afraid," not "You are wrong for making me feel this."
- Seek understanding, not control: ask for reassurance, agreements, and transparency.
- Work on inner wounds (abandonment, comparison, unworthiness).

Jealousy becomes misaligned when it leads to **control, punishment, or emotional blackmail**.

Aligned jealousy says: "I own my feelings and invite us to navigate them together."

Q4: *How much disclosure is required in polyamory to stay in The Way?*

A: The Way rejects **strategic vagueness** and half-truths. At minimum:

- All core partners should know polyamory is being practiced.
- No one should be misled about the existence or importance of other partners.
- Health, safety, and emotional risk must be discussed openly.

However, The Way does not require graphic detail or invasion of privacy.

The measure is: "Do they have enough truth to give *informed* consent and protect their heart and health?" If not, more truth is needed.

Q5: *Can hierarchies (primary/secondary partners) be compatible with The Way?*

A: Yes, if they are **explicit, consensual, and compassionate**.

- Everyone must understand their role and what it does and does not include.

- No one should be promised "eventual promotion" as a way to keep them hooked.

- Primary status should not be used as a weapon; secondary status should not mean "less human."

The Way calls for **honored differences**, not hidden hierarchies. Unspoken hierarchies are a form of deception, and thus are not aligned.

SWINGING AND RECREATIONAL INTIMACY

Swinging, within The Way of Still Waters, is the *consensual sharing of sexual experiences with others* for enjoyment, novelty, exploration, or connection — without seeking additional romantic bonds.

It is not casual chaos, nor is it a loophole around monogamy. It is a sophisticated relational structure requiring **truth, consent, clarity, emotional steadiness, and mutual respect**.

When practiced with discipline, swinging can strengthen connection, deepen trust, and expand intimacy. When practiced without discipline, it fractures stability, erodes safety, and invites dishonor.

---

1. THE ESSENCE OF SWINGING IN THE WAY

Doctrine

Swinging is consensual recreational sexuality, chosen together by a committed pair or autonomous individuals, governed by shared rules and upheld through respect, honesty, and emotional awareness.

Its purpose is:

- shared experience
- joyful exploration
- novelty without betrayal
- mutual enjoyment

- sexual expansion

Its power comes from:

- communication
- trust
- clear boundaries
- emotional grounding

It becomes misaligned when it conceals relational fractures or is used as a substitute for emotional connection.

———————

2. WHEN SWINGING ALIGNS WITH THE WAY

Swinging is compatible with The Way when it is:

A. MUTUALLY DESIRED

Both partners genuinely want this — not one dragging the other forward through subtle pressure, fear of loss, or guilt.

B. CO-CREATED THROUGH CLEAR AGREEMENTS

Boundaries, rules, and comfort zones must be:

- discussed
- respected
- revisited
- upheld with integrity

Agreements should cover:

- who
- where
- with whom

- frequency
- sexual acts
- communication before/during/after
- safety practices
- emotional aftercare

Conducted wth Full Transparency

- No secrets.
- No silent exceptions.
- No "rules apply unless I'm the one tempted."

Transparency is the backbone of trust.

Practiced from Emotional Stability

Swinging must come from a foundation of:

- security
- trust
- emotional maturity

It must not be used to:

- fix a fractured relationship
- distract from unresolved conflict
- fill emotional voids
- escape intimacy

Managed with Respect for All Participants

Partners and outside participants must be treated with:

- dignity

- kindness
- consent
- safe practices
- clear expectations

The Way forbids using others as objects, props, or placeholders.

---

3. WHEN SWINGING BECOMES MISALIGNED WITH THE WAY

Swinging drifts outside The Way when:

ONE PARTNER ISN'T TRULY COMFORTABLE

If someone "agrees" out of:

- fear
- insecurity
- pressure
- wanting to "keep up"
- fear of abandonment

Then swinging becomes emotional self-betrayal.

IT MASKS OR AVOIDS RELATIONSHIP PROBLEMS

If swinging is used to:

- avoid hard conversations
- escape intimacy
- compensate for emotional distance
- distract from relational pain

It is misaligned because the foundation is already fractured.

BOUNDARIES ARE BROKEN OR BENT

Rules that are ignored "just this once" or "because the moment carried you away" destroy trust.

Breaking a boundary in swinging is a form of betrayal.

JEALOUSY IS IGNORED OR MINIMIZED

Jealousy is not a flaw — it is an emotional signal. Dismissing it or shaming it is misaligned.

The Way requires addressing it with compassion and strategy, not denial.

IT BECOMES A SOURCE OF CHAOS

Swinging becomes misaligned when it:

- destabilizes the primary relationship
- creates emotional wounds
- causes secrecy
- leads to resentment
- introduces conflict that is minimized or dismissed

Pleasure must not create destruction.

---

4. THE UNIQUE ETHICAL DEMANDS OF SWINGING

Swinging has its own set of disciplines distinct from monogamy or polyamory:

PRECISION OF AGREEMENTS

Because swinging is event-based, rules must be precise.

EMOTIONAL REGULATION

Partners must know their triggers, tolerances, and thresholds.

POST-EXPERIENCE PROCESSING

Aftercare is essential:

- checking in
- emotional connection
- reassurance
- recalibration

CONSISTENCY OF CONDUCT

Do not change the rules mid-experience or surprise your partner with new behaviors.

EQUAL PARTICIPATION

Neither partner should be consistently sidelined, pressured, or overshadowed.

---

5. TYPES OF SWINGING AND THEIR ALIGNMENT

SOFT-SWAP SWINGING (NON-PENETRATIVE)

Aligned when both agree on limits. Misaligned when used as a stepping stone without consent.

FULL-SWAP SWINGING

Aligned when:

- both partners are fully comfortable
- aftercare is prioritized

Misaligned if:

- boundaries are stretched without discussion
- one partner is trying to "prove" something

SAME-ROOM VS. SEPARATE-ROOM SWINGING

Aligned when:

- the choice matches comfort levels
- transparency is maintained

Misaligned if:

- Separate rooms become a loophole for secrecy
- one partner is excluded from truths they should know

SOLO PLAY

Aligned when:

- openly discussed
- fully consented to
- emotionally safe

Misaligned when:

- used to pursue personal desires the partner would reject
- used to imitate discreet cheating

GROUP OR PARTY-BASED SWINGING

Aligned when:

- partners feel secure
- boundaries are maintained even in dynamic settings

Misaligned when:

- partners feel abandoned or emotionally unsafe in groups

---

6. THE FIVE ETHICAL QUESTIONS OF SWINGING

Q1: Are we doing this from connection, or running from something?

If you are escaping a problem, swinging will magnify it.

Q2: Do we both feel equally excited and safe?

If one is enthusiastic and one is tolerating, the dynamic is misaligned.

Q3: Are our rules clear enough to prevent emotional confusion?

Ambiguity is the seed of betrayal.

Q4: What emotional support will we offer each other before and after?

Swinging is easier on the body than the heart — aftercare matters.

Q5: Does swinging enhance our bond, or slowly erode it?

Track the pattern, not a single event.

---

7. CORE DOCTRINE OF SWINGING IN THE WAY

"Recreational intimacy requires disciplined integrity."

"Pleasure is aligned only when it harms none, hides nothing, and honors all involved."

"Do nothing in the moment that you would regret in the morning."

"Swinging must expand connection, not fracture it."

Swinging

Compatible if:

- It is recreational, consensual, and ethically practiced.
- Both partners participate without coercion, guilt, or imBalance.
- Rules are made *together* and honored *strictly*.
- It strengthens communication and trust rather than eroding it.
- It does not entangle outside people in dishonesty.

Incompatible if:

- One partner secretly dislikes it but "goes along."
- It becomes escapism from unresolved relational issues.
- It introduces chaos, jealousy, dishonor, or secrecy.
- It is used to mask infidelity under a false veneer of consent.

The Way's Verdict:

Swinging can be compatible *only when done with maturity, transparency, and Balance.*

SWINGING — ADDITIONAL QUESTIONS

Q1: Is it aligned with The Way to try swinging "just to spice things up" in a struggling relationship?

A: If swinging is used as a **distraction from unresolved wounds**, it is misaligned.

- The Way insists: repair first, then experiment.
- If trust is already fragile, adding more variables often deepens harm.

Before swinging, The Way would ask:

"Are we doing this from a place of connection, or trying to cover a fracture with novelty?"

Novelty cannot replace emotional repair.

Q2: What if one partner enjoys swinging far more than the other?

A: Difference in enjoyment is not automatically misaligned; **pressure is**.

- The Way requires that "no" is always a valid, respected answer.
- If one partner feels obligated, guilty, or fears abandonment for declining, consent is not truly free.

An aligned path:

- Name the difference.
- Explore compromises that **do not** cost either person their self-respect or safety.

Where peace cannot be found without one person shrinking, The Way may gently suggest reevaluating the entire arrangement.

Q3: Is secrecy about swinging from friends or family a violation of The Way?

A: The Way distinguishes between **privacy** and **deception**.

- Privacy: "Our consensual choices are not everyone's business."
- Deception: lying when directly asked, or constructing elaborate false stories that entangle others.

The Way does not require you to announce your sex life to the world; it simply forbids **dragging others into webs of lies**.

Q4: How should boundaries with recurring swinging partners be handled?

A: Recurring partners blur lines between "purely recreational" and "relational." The Way requires:

- Periodic check-ins: "Has this dynamic shifted for anyone?"
- Agreed limits: emotional, physical, communicational.
- Attention to attachment and jealousy signals.

If recurring connections start to create **unspoken emotional entanglements**, continuing without addressing it strays from The Way, because silence here becomes a form of dishonesty.

Q5: Is it aligned with The Way to swing under the influence of alcohol or substances?

A: The Way values **clarity of consent and awareness**.

- Mild relaxation is one thing; decision-impairing intoxication is another.
- If someone is too impaired to reliably consent, any sexual activity is out of alignment.

The guideline: "If they couldn't clearly recount or own the choice tomorrow, it is not truly in The Way today."

FRIENDS WITH BENEFITS AND CASUAL CONNECTION

Friends with Benefits (FWB) and casual intimacy are valid relational forms within The Way of Still Waters, but they require **more honesty with oneself** than perhaps any other structure.

Romantic bonds have frameworks.
Monogamy has vows.
Polyamory has agreements.
Swinging has rules.

Casual connections often have **nothing but truth and boundaries** between two hearts. Without these, casual becomes careless — and careless becomes harmful.

This section codifies how casual intimacy aligns or misaligns with The Way.

----

1. THE ESSENCE OF FWB & CASUAL INTIMACY IN THE WAY

DOCTRINE

FWB and casual intimacy are relationships defined by:

- mutual enjoyment
- shared attraction
- emotional connection without exclusive commitment
- honesty about expectations
- respect for each other's sovereignty
- freedom from romantic obligation

Casual is not "less than." Casual is simply **different**, and requires its own ethical clarity.

The key to alignment is **truth of intent** — your own and the other person's.

---

2. WHEN FWB & CASUAL CONNECTION ALIGN WITH THE WAY

These connections align when both partners:

SHARE THE SAME INTENTION

Both must genuinely desire a casual dynamic — not secretly hope it evolves, not reluctantly accept it, not pretend comfort they do not feel.

Misalignment begins at the first unspoken hope.

COMMUNICATE EXPECTATIONS OPENLY

Before intimacy deepens, clarity must be spoken:

- What is this?
- What is it not?
- What level of emotional support is expected?
- Is exclusivity expected or not?
- How often will communication occur?
- Are sleepovers, dates, or emotional closeness allowed?

FWB fails when expectations differ but remain unspoken.

MAINTAIN KINDNESS WITHOUT PRETENDING ROMANTIC COMMITMENT

The Way forbids cruelty, manipulation, and emotional exploitation. It does not require romantic dedication where none was promised.

You must be:

- kind
- honest
- considerate

Not:

- misleading
- ambiguous
- inconsistent to keep someone attached

PROTECT THE EMOTIONAL AND PHYSICAL HEALTH OF BOTH PARTNERS

Safety in all forms (sexual, emotional, logistical) is essential.

Aligned partners:

- disclose relevant information truthfully
- practice safe intimacy
- avoid exposing one another to relational chaos
- are mindful of emotional shifts

ALLOW THE CONNECTION TO EVOLVE OR END WITHOUT PUNISHMENT

FWB works only when both partners:

- allow emotional truth to shift
- can renegotiate or conclude the dynamic
- honor changes without blame
- release the bond gracefully if the heart changes

Casual requires **emotional maturity**, not emotional detachment.

3. WHEN FWB & CASUAL DYNAMICS MISALIGN WITH THE WAY

Casual intimacy leaves the path when:

ONE PERSON SECRETLY WANTS MORE

If someone hopes it will "turn into something," but hides that truth to keep access to intimacy, they violate both Truth and Honor — inwardly and outwardly.

Self-betrayal is still betrayal.

ONE PERSON USES THE OTHER FOR EMOTIONAL SUBSTITUTION

Using someone for:

- loneliness relief
- validation
- attention
- avoiding heartbreak
- avoiding healing

Always creates harm, even if they agree to the connection.

Intent matters.

EMOTIONAL PAIN IS IGNORED OR MINIMIZED

If one person is hurting and the other says:

- "Well, you knew what this was,"
  or
- "That's your problem, not mine,"

This violates Compassion and Honor.

Casual does not exempt someone from responsibility.

BOUNDARIES ARE NOT RESPECTED

FWB becomes misaligned when:

- one person begins texting excessively
- one expects emotional labor not agreed upon
- one seeks exclusivity through pressure
- intimacy creeps into romantic territory without discussion

Casual requires vigilance.

COMMUNICATION BECOMES INCONSISTENT OR WEAPONIZED

If one person:

- disappears for long periods
- breadcrumbs attention
- uses silence to control access
- manipulates connection timing

The dynamic is no longer casual — it is harmful.

---

4. THE UNIQUE ETHICAL DEMANDS OF FWB & CASUAL CONNECTION

FWB is deceptively simple but ethically complex.

These relationships require:

HIGH SELF-AWARENESS

You must know:

- your attachment patterns
- your triggers
- your needs

- your limits

Casual is not for those who confuse intensity with intimacy.

EMOTIONAL HONESTY WITH YOURSELF

Ask:

- Am I truly okay with this?
- Am I hoping it becomes more?
- Am I using this person to fill an emptiness?

If the truth is painful to admit, it is necessary to admit.

STEADY COMMUNICATION

FWB collapses not from conflict, but from silence.

CAPACITY TO HANDLE CHANGE

At any moment:

- someone may meet someone else
- someone may catch feelings
- someone may lose feelings
- someone may need more distance

Casual requires flexibility — without guilt or punishment.

CLEAN ENDINGS

FWB must end with clarity, not ghosting.

Ghosting violates:

- Truth
- Honor

- Responsibility
- Compassion
- No Harm

Closure is respect.

---

5. TYPES OF CASUAL DYNAMICS AND THEIR ALIGNMENT

TRUE FWB (FRIENDSHIP + SEXUAL INTIMACY)

Aligned when:

- friendship remains intact
- clarity of boundaries is maintained
- care is given without romantic expectations

Misaligned when:

- one person uses sex to gain emotional closeness
- friendship becomes an excuse for possession

CASUAL ENCOUNTERS (ONE-TIME OR OCCASIONAL)

Aligned when:

- intentions are mutual
- boundaries are clear
- communication is respectful

Misaligned when:

- someone is intoxicated beyond ability to consent
- one person is used as emotional anesthesia

SITUATIONSHIPS

(Where neither is willing to define the dynamic)

Aligned only when:

- both truly prefer that ambiguity
- both can function without clarity

Misaligned when:

- one wants more definition
- the ambiguity is a cloak for emotional avoidance
- someone is being strung along

RECURRING CASUAL PARTNER

Aligned when:

- emotional attachment is monitored
- expectations remain unchanged
- transparency about outside partners continues

Misaligned when:

- emotional intimacy grows without acknowledgment
- one partner becomes "accidentally exclusive"

TRANSITIONAL FWB

(where one or both partners are healing from a breakup)

Aligned when:

- both know this is temporary
- emotional boundaries are strong

Misaligned when:

- the FWB is used to avoid grief
- the partner becomes a stand-in for the ex
- false hope is generated

---

6. Five Ethical Questions of FWB & Casual Connection

Q1: Am I genuinely content with this level of connection?

If the answer is not steady and honest, the dynamic is not aligned.

Q2: Am I showing up with kindness even without commitment?

Casual is not a license for coldness.

Q3: Am I misleading them about my intentions?

If yes, the connection has already breached Truth and Honor.

Q4: Is this helping me grow or keeping me stuck?

The purpose of the dynamic must be examined periodically.

Q5: If this ended today, would I regret my conduct?

This is the compass of Honor.

---

7. CORE DOCTRINE OF FWB & CASUAL INTIMACY

"Casual does not mean careless."

"Freedom of connection does not excuse harm."

"Casual intimacy is sustained not by romance, but by clarity, kindness, and truth."

"Where honesty ends, casual becomes cruelty."

FRIENDS WITH BENEFITS

Compatible if:

- Both people are genuinely aligned in expectations.
- No one is being used to fill an emotional void.
- No one is misleading the other about their intentions.
- The arrangement does not foster attachment that one side denies.
- Emotional safety is prioritized.

Incompatible if:

- Feelings grow unspoken.
- One person is uncared for or treated dismissively.
- It becomes a substitute for emotional intimacy while claiming "no strings."

The Way's Verdict:
FWB is only aligned if both hearts are genuinely steady and no one is being diminished by participating.

Friends With Benefits — Additional Questions

Q1: Can a FWB arrangement evolve into a romantic relationship and stay aligned with The Way?

A: Yes — if **honesty evolves with the feelings**.

- When emotions deepen, the agreement must be updated.
- Saying nothing and hoping the other "figures it out" is not The Way.

Alignment path: "My feelings have shifted. I need to talk about what this is for me now, even if it risks the current comfort."

Courageous truth honors both hearts.

Q2: What if one person secretly hopes FWB will "turn into more," while the other clearly stated they don't want that?

A: The Way requires internal honesty:

- If you cannot genuinely accept the terms, continuing becomes self-betrayal.
- Self-betrayal is still a form of harm, even if the other did "nothing wrong."

The ethical step is to either:

- Reopen the conversation and share your new truth, or
- Step away to protect your heart.

Staying in a situation that steadily erodes you is not walking in The Way.

Q3: Is it aligned with The Way to have multiple FWB partners at once?

A: Potentially, if:

- Everyone is informed that this is non-exclusive.
- Sexual health and safety are proactively managed.
- No one is being led to believe they are "the only one" if they are not.

Misalignment appears when you present a **false picture of exclusivity** to gain emotional access or compliance. The Way forbids that.

Q4: How does The Way view emotional detachment in FWB?

A: The Way favors **integration, not numbness**.

- If "no feelings" is actually emotional shutdown, self-numbing, or avoidance of intimacy, the arrangement is misaligned with inner truth.

- If both are naturally capable of warm, respectful connection without romantic bonding, that can be aligned.

The inner question: "Am I genuinely okay, or am I silencing my deeper needs to keep this convenient?"

Q5: When is it time to end a FWB situation according to The Way?

A: It is time to release when:

- You feel consistently diminished, anxious, or unseen.

- Your needs have changed and are not being met.

- The arrangement obstructs you from pursuing the kind of relationship you truly desire.

The Way teaches: "Release with clarity and kindness, rather than lingering in quiet suffering."

Endings are not failures; they are course corrections toward alignment.

CHEATING, BETRAYAL, AND THE PATH BACK TO HONOR

Cheating is the act most fundamentally opposed to The Way of Still Waters. Not because of its sexual nature, but because it violates the four pillars most sacred to relational conduct:

Truth. Honor. Consent. No Harm.

Where monogamy, polyamory, swinging, and casual intimacy can all align with The Way through honesty and consent, cheating stands apart as the one relational choice defined *entirely* by deception.

This section establishes The Way's doctrine on betrayal, its mechanics, its consequences, and the path — if chosen — back to honor.

---

1. WHAT CHEATING IS ACCORDING TO THE WAY

DOCTRINE

Cheating is:

- a conscious violation of agreement
- paired with the deliberate concealment of that violation
- resulting in the erosion of trust, dignity, and consent

It is not the act of touching another person.
It is the act of **lying** about touching another person.
It is the secret world that wounds, not the body that strays.

Cheating is **the theft of someone's ability to choose**.

---

2. WHY CHEATING VIOLATES THE WAY

Cheating violates:

Truth

It creates a false reality and asks another to live inside it.

Honor

It treats the partner not as sovereign but as someone to be managed.

Consent

It removes the partner's right to make informed choices.

Compassion

It disregards the emotional impact.

Responsibility

It deflects accountability until discovery.

Balance

It destabilizes the foundation of connection.

No Harm

It causes deep emotional injury, often in silence.

Cheating, by definition, cannot align with The Way because it depends on hiding, minimizing, or distorting truth.

---

3. FORMS OF BETRAYAL

Cheating is not only sexual. The Way distinguishes four categories:

SEXUAL INFIDELITY

Engaging sexually with another person outside agreed boundaries.

The harm:

- broken agreement
- hidden risk
- concealed intimacy

EMOTIONAL INFIDELITY

Secret emotional bonding that replaces or competes with the primary relationship's intimacy.

The harm:

- secrecy
- emotional displacement
- romantic energy used elsewhere

If you must hide it, it is betrayal.

DIGITAL OR FANTASY-BASED INFIDELITY

Sexting, explicit chats, secret OnlyFans subscriptions, hidden online personas, or romantic interactions behind a partner's back.

The harm:

- emotional investment
- broken boundaries

- concealed sexual energy

Digital does not make it less real.

Even without physical or emotional contact, the act of lying about:

- desires
- intentions
- boundaries
- communication with someone else

…can constitute cheating when the deception removes informed consent.

The Way judges betrayal by the **truth concealed**, not only the act committed.

---

4. THE ANATOMY OF BETRAYAL

Betrayal has three moving parts:

The Act

What occurred.

The Lie

What was hidden?

The Wake

The harm radiating from the concealment.

While the act may be small, the lie is almost always larger.

---

5. WHEN SUSPICION ARISES: THE WAY'S GUIDANCE

The Way advises:

Ask for clarity, not confession-by-force.

State the concern directly and calmly.

Observe actions, not words alone.

Words guide; actions reveal.

Trust inner stillness, not fear's noise.

Stillness perceives truth. Fear imagines it.

Maintain self-honor regardless of outcome.

Do not pursue truth through dishonor.

---

6. Responses to Betrayal According to The Way

When betrayal is discovered, the injured partner may choose one of three aligned paths:

RELEASE

End the relationship with clarity and dignity.

Aligned because:

- it honors self
- it removes ongoing harm
- it closes the bond cleanly

RECONCILIATION (IF DESIRED)

Attempt repair through truth, accountability, and rebuilding.

Aligned only when:

- the betrayer fully confesses
- excuses stop
- patterns are confronted
- both partners commit to healing

Reconciliation is impossible without **radical transparency**.

TRANSFORMATION OF RELATIONSHIP STRUCTURE

(Only with true mutual desire)

Shifting to:

- ethical non-monogamy
- polyamory
- new agreements

This is *never* an immediate solution. It is possible only after deep repair.

Otherwise, it becomes a mask for continued betrayal.

---

7. THE PATH BACK TO HONOR (IF CHOSEN)

The Way offers redemption, but it is not cheap. The betrayer must walk a path of **seven disciplines**:

FULL ACKNOWLEDGMENT

No minimizing.
No "but nothing happened."
No emotional loopholes.

FULL TRANSPARENCY

Every meaningful detail that restores the partner's ability to choose must be shared.

ACCOUNTABILITY WITHOUT DEFENSE

No shifting blame.
No counter-accusing.
No self-victimization.

WILLINGNESS TO FACE CONSEQUENCES

The betrayed partner may leave — this must be accepted without anger.

CONSISTENT TRUTHFULNESS GOING FORWARD

Transparency becomes a practice, not a punishment.

REPAIR THROUGH ACTION

Changing:

- behaviors
- access
- boundaries
- digital habits
- emotional openness

Words alone cannot repair.

PATIENCE WITH THEIR HEALING

You cannot rush someone back to trust.

The betrayer must tolerate:

- their pain
- their questions
- their moments of doubt

Honor requires perseverance, not pressure.

8. THE BETRAYED PERSON'S PATH BACK TO SELF

The injured partner has their own disciplines:

Reclaim Self-Worth

Cheating reflects the betrayer's misalignment, not your inadequacy.

Choose Your Truth

You may stay or leave — either path is aligned if chosen with clarity.

Demand Accountability, Not Punishment

Punishment is not healing; honesty is.

Rebuild Autonomy

Your choices, boundaries, and pace of healing are sovereign.

Release Self-Blame

No one "causes" another to betray.

Pursue Inner Stillness

Heal before rebuilding — whether alone or together.

Reestablish Boundaries

Insist on new safeguards that protect your emotional landscape.

9. THE FIVE ETHICAL QUESTIONS OF BETRAYAL

Q1: Is the damage from the betrayal repairable?

Only when truth is complete and effort is mutual.

Q2: Is the remorse genuine or strategic?

Remorse transforms; strategy manipulates.

Q3: Does the betrayer seek redemption or absolution?

Redemption requires action. Absolution seeks escape.

Q4: Can trust be rebuilt without self-betrayal?

If rebuilding requires you to silence your truth, the answer is no.

Q5: What path leads to the most inner stillness?

This is the compass of The Way.

---

10. CORE DOCTRINE OF CHEATING & BETRAYAL

"Cheating is not the breaking of exclusivity. It is the breaking of truth."

"The wound of betrayal lies not in the act, but in the secret world built behind your back."

"A relationship may survive betrayal — but only if deceit does not survive with it."

"Honor lost can be regained only through truth, responsibility, and sustained change."

ETHICAL NON-MONOGAMY VS. CHEATING

Ethical non-monogamy may align with The Way when built on:

- Truth
- Mutual consent
- Honor
- Responsibility

- Balance
- Compassion

Cheating is never compatible with The Way.

The Codex makes a *very* clear distinction:

- **Cheating = incompatible with The Way.**
  It violates honor, truth, consent, compassion, non-harm, and the sovereign dignity of the other.
- **Ethical non-monogamy = potentially compatible.**
  It is built on truth, consent, boundaries, and mindful conduct.

The Way judges **behavioral integrity**, not the structure.

ETHICAL NON-MONOGAMY VS. CHEATING — ADDITIONAL QUESTIONS

Q1: Is it still cheating if "there were no feelings, it was just physical"?

A: Yes. Cheating is defined by **betrayal of agreed boundaries**, not by emotional content.

- If exclusivity was promised, then any sexual engagement outside that promise, hidden or denied, is cheating.
- "No feelings" does not cleanse the dishonor; it only changes the flavor of the wound.

The Way sees the broken word, not just the broken heart.

Q2: What if my partner says, "I don't want to know what you do, just don't tell me"? Is that ethical non-monogamy?

A: This is a gray and dangerous edge.

- If this boundary was truly discussed, understood, and freely chosen, it *may* be aligned — but it is fragile.
- Often, this posture hides avoidance: "I can't handle the truth, but I also don't want to set a clear boundary."

The Way prefers **conscious consent** over willful ignorance. If "don't tell me" is actually "I will pretend not to know so I don't have to act," it is not fully aligned.

Q3: Can cheating ever be "redeemed" and brought back into The Way?

A: Yes — but not lightly, and not quickly. It requires:

- Full acknowledgment of the betrayal with no minimizing.
- Transparent truth about what happened and why.
- Willingness to accept consequences, including the possibility of the relationship ending.
- Active, sustained work to rebuild trust.

The Way allows for **restoration**, but never at the cost of the injured party's autonomy. They are not obligated to forgive, reconcile, or remain.

Q4: Is hiding emotional intimacy with someone else (but not being physical) a form of cheating?

A: This is often called **emotional infidelity**. The Way examines:

- Were boundaries about emotional exclusivity ever discussed?
- Are you deliberately concealing the depth of this connection from your partner?
- Would you feel comfortable if your partner saw every message or knew every detail?

If you are building a secret world with someone else that you know would wound your partner, you are already stepping outside The Way — even without physical touch.

Q5: How do I transition from cheating patterns to ethical non-monogamy in alignment with The Way?

A: This is a **hard reset**, not a rebrand.

Steps aligned with The Way:

1. **Stop the deceit now.** No new secrets.
2. **Confess honestly** — not every graphic detail, but the real scope and pattern.
3. **Accept the impact** and the other person's right to leave.
4. If the relationship continues, **rebuild from truth**:

   ○ Re-negotiate boundaries.

   ○ Possibly explore open or poly structures, but *only* after significant healing and with mutual desire — not as a forced "solution."

The Way does not grant a shortcut from betrayal to "ethical" non-monogamy. The road passes through **truth, accountability, and repair** first.

EMOTIONAL AFFAIRS AND ATTACHMENT BOUNDARIES

Emotional affairs occur not in the body, but in the heart. They are formed where intimacy deepens in secret, where truth becomes selectively withheld, and where emotional energy is redirected into a private bond beyond the agreed relationship. The Way of Still Waters does not define betrayal by the behavior itself, but by the **deception**, the **displacement of intimacy**, and the **erosion of trust** that grows in silence.

This section establishes how emotional affairs form, why they violate The Way, and how to create healthy attachment boundaries.

1. WHAT AN EMOTIONAL AFFAIR IS ACCORDING TO THE WAY

DOCTRINE

An emotional affair is a relationship — often cloaked in friendship — that becomes a private world of intimacy, affection, or attachment that is concealed from one's partner.

It may or may not include sexual attraction. It may or may not include explicit intimacy.

But it always includes:

- secrecy
- emotional displacement
- a specialness hidden from one's partner

The Way defines an emotional affair by:

- **the hide,**
- **the emotional prioritization,**
- **the protective secrecy,**
- and the **inner knowing that the partner would be hurt**.

If you would not show the messages or conversations to your partner, the affair has already begun.

---

2. WHY EMOTIONAL AFFAIRS VIOLATE THE WAY

Emotional betrayal violates:

Truth

Because important emotional realities are hidden.

Honor

Because loyalty is diverted into secrecy.

Consent

Because a partner loses the ability to understand the emotional landscape of the relationship.

Compassion

Because vulnerability is given privately while the partner is kept in the dark.

Balance

Because the emotional center of gravity shifts; priorities alter without transparency.

No Harm

Because emotional betrayal deeply wounds, often more profoundly than sexual betrayal.

Secrecy is the harm. Not the conversation.

---

3. SIGNS AN EMOTIONAL AFFAIR HAS FORMED

These are the indicators The Way considers meaningful:

You hide the depth of the connection.

If you conceal details, frequency, or tone, the boundary is already breached.

You turn to them for emotional comfort before your partner.

The emotional bond has shifted.

You fantasize about them as an escape from your relationship.

This is displacement, not harmless daydreaming.

You share private frustrations about your partner with them.

This creates intimacy through triangulation.

You romanticize the emotional bond or protect it from scrutiny.

If the connection feels "separate" or "special," the line is crossed.

You would feel threatened if your partner knew the full extent.

Secrecy reveals truth.

---

4. Attachment Boundaries in The Way

Attachment boundaries are not barriers to friendship; they are the structures that ensure emotional intimacy is aligned, transparent, and respectful.

The Way recommends:

TRANSPARENCY, NOT POLICING

You do not need permission for every connection — but alignment requires openness.

EMOTIONAL SAFETY

Ask:
"Would this hurt my partner if they knew?"
If yes, slow down and re-center.

PREVENTING INTIMACY DRIFT

Emotional drift occurs when:

- affection
- admiration
- comfort
- vulnerability
- shared secrets

…begin to resemble romantic connection.

This must be addressed early, kindly, and honestly.

MAINTAINING THE PRIMACY OF THE CHOSEN BOND

In monogamous or hierarchical structures, the primary partner must not become emotionally displaced or demoted without consent.

PROTECTING THE CONNECTION FROM TRIANGULATION

Do not:

- vent complaints to someone new
- use friendship to avoid conflict
- build intimacy around shared dissatisfaction

Triangulation creates false closeness and real harm.

---

5. WHEN A FRIENDSHIP IS ALIGNED VS. WHEN IT BECOMES AN EMOTIONAL AFFAIR

ALIGNED FRIENDSHIP:

- Your partner knows about the friendship.
- The tone is respectful and non-flirtatious.
- You maintain consistent emotional availability in your relationship.
- Boundaries are clear and honored.
- Nothing is hidden.
- You would show your partner the full conversation without fear.

EMOTIONAL AFFAIR:

- Conversations are hidden or minimized.
- Emotional energy shifts toward the other person.
- You share more of your heart with them than your partner.
- You feel guilt — or excitement — about the secrecy.
- You protect the connection from your partner's awareness.
- You fantasize about what "might be."

The dividing line is secrecy.

---

6. WHAT TO DO WHEN EMOTIONAL DRIFT BEGINS

The Way advises:

Slow the connection.

Do not feed the fire.

Reinvest in the primary bond.

Put emotional energy back where it belongs.

Name the drift honestly to yourself.

Self-deception precedes betrayal.

Set or reset boundaries.

Adjust communication frequency, tone, or topic.

If appropriate, share the concern with your partner.

Transparency restores trust.

Emotional drift is not betrayal yet — but silence makes it so.

---

7. HEALING AFTER AN EMOTIONAL AFFAIR

Both partners have roles:

FOR THE ONE WHO FORMED THE BOND

1. Confess fully, without minimizing.
2. Cut or radically alter the inappropriate connection.
3. Clean up digital, emotional, and logistical access.
4. Return emotional availability to your partner.
5. Be patient during their healing.

6. Rebuild trust through action, not promises.

FOR THE INJURED PARTNER

1. Name the pain without self-blame.
2. Decide if reconciliation is desired.
3. Set new boundaries that protect trust.
4. Ask for honesty, but not surveillance.
5. Rebuild your own inner stability.

Healing is not instantaneous. But with truth, consistency, and compassion, it is possible.

---

8. THE FIVE QUESTIONS OF EMOTIONAL ALIGNMENT

Q1: Would I say this if my partner were here?

If not, realign.

Q2: Am I turning away from my partner to turn toward another?

This requires immediate attention.

Q3: Am I hiding the emotional significance of this bond?

Secrecy is the litmus test.

Q4: Does this connection nourish or destabilize my primary relationship?

Choose alignment over intensity.

Q5: What does my inner stillness say?

The Way speaks through honesty, not rationalization.

---

9. CORE DOCTRINE OF EMOTIONAL AFFAIRS IN THE WAY

"Betrayal begins in the heart long before it reaches the body."

"Secrets create worlds where partners cannot follow — and that is the wound."

"Friendship aligns. Secrecy corrupts. Transparency restores."

"Every bond must be tended in the light."

THE SIXFOLD ALIGNMENT TEST

The Sixfold Alignment Test is the core evaluative tool of The Way of Still Waters. It is used to assess **any** relational situation — monogamous, polyamorous, casual, conflicted, broken, or undefined.

Every choice, action, omission, boundary, desire, or dilemma can be tested through these six lenses:

Truth — Honor — Responsibility — Compassion — Balance — No Harm

When all six align, the path is clear. When even one fails, the situation requires correction, conversation, or release.

Below is the fully developed test, with doctrine, applications, and guiding questions.

1. TRUTH — "IS THIS CLEAN, OR IS IT HIDDEN?"

DOCTRINE

Truth is the foundation of consent, trust, and clear connection. Anything concealed that affects another's ability to choose is misaligned.

ALIGNED WHEN:

- All partners have the information they need
- Intentions are spoken, not implied
- There is no deception by silence or omission

- Motives and feelings are expressed honestly

- You are hiding something meaningful
- You rationalize secrecy
- You tell partial truths to shape perception
- You rely on ambiguity to avoid accountability

- Am I being completely honest — with them and myself?
- Would I be willing to tell this truth openly?
- Am I hiding anything that could change their choices?
- Does this create clarity or confusion?

---

2. HONOR — "DOES THIS UPHOLD DIGNITY, OR DIMINISH IT?"

DOCTRINE

Honor recognizes the sovereignty of every heart. It treats others not as tools or conveniences, but as equal beings deserving dignity.

ALIGNED WHEN:

- You respect their boundaries, needs, and identity
- Your actions match your promises
- You value their humanity, not just their company
- You protect the bond from disrespect

MISALIGNED WHEN:

- You manipulate, pressure, or coerce

- You treat someone as replaceable or lesser
- You disguise selfishness as "freedom"
- You violate agreements or trust

GUIDING QUESTIONS:

- Does this uphold their dignity?
- Does it uphold mine?
- Am I being the person I would trust if roles were reversed?
- Will I be proud of this choice tomorrow?

---

3. RESPONSIBILITY — "AM I OWNING THE EFFECTS OF THIS?"

DOCTRINE

Responsibility means acknowledging not only your intentions, but the **impact** of your actions.

ALIGNED WHEN:

- You take accountability without excuses
- You repair harm where possible
- You manage your insecurities and emotional triggers
- You keep your word consistently

MISALIGNED WHEN:

- You blame others for your choices
- You minimize harm you caused
- You avoid difficult conversations
- You deflect accountability through anger or withdrawal

- What is the real impact of my choice?
- Am I taking responsibility, or making excuses?
- What must I do to repair or prevent harm?
- Am I acting with maturity or avoidance?

---

4. COMPASSION — "DOES THIS CARE FOR THE HEART INVOLVED?"

DOCTRINE

Compassion aligns action with empathy. It weighs emotional impact and refuses to cause unnecessary suffering.

ALIGNED WHEN:

- You express truth kindly
- You consider their emotional landscape
- You treat vulnerability with gentleness
- You choose timing and tone with care

MISALIGNED WHEN:

- You weaponize truth
- You mock or dismiss their feelings
- You withhold affection as punishment
- You use emotional leverage to get your way

GUIDING QUESTIONS:

- Does this action consider their feelings?
- Am I choosing kindness without sacrificing honesty?
- What is the most humane way to proceed?

- Does this help or wound?

---

5. BALANCE — "DOES THIS SUSTAIN STABILITY, OR CREATE CHAOS?"

DOCTRINE

Balance means neither losing yourself to connection nor withholding connection out of fear.

ALIGNED WHEN:

- Your boundaries are clear and consistent
- You give without overextending
- You receive without taking advantage
- Your choices bring calm, not chaos

MISALIGNED WHEN:

- You cling or withdraw excessively
- You sacrifice your identity for connection
- You use people to avoid loneliness
- You create instability, jealousy, or confusion

GUIDING QUESTIONS:

- Does this add stability or turbulence?
- Am I grounded, or am I reacting from fear?
- Am I giving too much? Too little?
- Is this choice in Balance with who I am?

---

6. NO HARM — "DOES THIS DIMINISH ANYONE INVOLVED?"

DOCTRINE

No Harm is not about avoiding discomfort — it is about avoiding **damage**.

Discomfort may be necessary for truth; harm is never necessary for connection.

ALIGNED WHEN:

- Your choices avoid unnecessary injury
- You refuse to exploit vulnerability
- You end situations that repeatedly wound
- You protect both yourself and others

MISALIGNED WHEN:

- You knowingly cause pain to protect yourself
- You remain in dynamics that corrode your spirit
- You prioritize pleasure over safety
- You allow harm through silence or inaction

GUIDING QUESTIONS:

- Does this cause harm or healing?
- Am I tolerating what diminishes me?
- Who is hurt by this choice?
- Is the harm avoidable?

THE COMPLETE SIXFOLD ALIGNMENT TEST (QUICK VERSION)

To evaluate any relational decision, ask:

1. **Truth:** Is this fully honest?
2. **Honor:** Does this preserve dignity?
3. **Responsibility:** Am I owning the impact?
4. **Compassion:** Is this kind as well as honest?
5. **Balance:** Does this maintain stability?
6. **No Harm:** Does this avoid unnecessary damage?

If the answer is "no" to even one pillar, **pause, correct, or choose another path.**

THE SIXFOLD TEST OF ALIGNMENT

Every form of relationship — monogamy, polyamory, swinging, FWB — must pass the **Sixfold Test of The Way**:

1. **Truth:** Is everyone fully informed and unmisled?
2. **Honor:** Is no one being misled, manipulated, or deprived of dignity? Is dignity upheld for all involved?
3. **Responsibility:** Are consequences owned and managed rather than avoided?
4. **Compassion:** Does this care for all hearts involved? Are hearts cared for, not exploited or ignored?
5. **Balance:** Does this cultivate peace, not chaos?
6. **No Harm:** Does this avoid diminishing anyone, including oneself?

Failing even one of these consistently moves the relationship outside The Way.

CORE DOCTRINE

"Any path walked with open truth, shared consent, and compassionate responsibility aligns with The Way. Any path walked in secrecy, deception, or harm does not."

The Way is about **how you love**, not the format in which you love.

"TO RISE ANEW, YOU MUST LOOSEN YOUR HOLD ON THE OLD."

THE JOURNEY BEGINS...

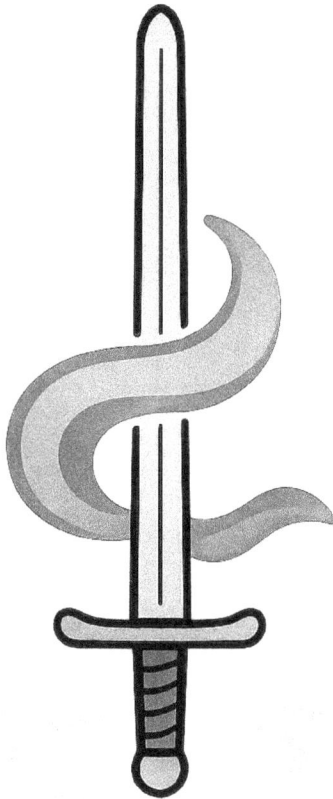

A new beginning rarely arrives with certainty.
It arrives with a small, persistent whisper that you can no longer ignore.

You don't need to know the whole path
to take the first honest step toward it.

"Beginnings are born the moment you stop standing still."

IN CONCLUSION: WALKING THE WAY

There comes a point in every path where study must become movement.
Reflection must become practice.
Principle must become presence.

The Way of Still Waters was never meant to be memorized; it was meant to be lived.
Not as a performance of virtue, not as a rigid doctrine, but as a quiet daily alignment of intention, action, and awareness.

In a world that often rewards noise over clarity, force over wisdom, and impulse over integrity, choosing stillness is an act of courage. Choosing compassion is an act of strength. Choosing truth is an act of honor.

This Codex has given you the structure —
Steel for right action, Water for right relationship, Balance for right awareness.
It has given you the virtues, the daily practices, the relational ethics, and the Sixfold Alignment Test.

Now the question becomes simple:

How will you walk from here?

THE WAY IS CHOSEN IN MOMENTS, NOT MILESTONES

The Way is not reached by grand gestures, nor earned by perfection.
It is revealed in the small choices:

- The difficult truth spoken with kindness.
- The boundary held without cruelty.
- The apology offered without excuses.
- The courage to act when silence would cost someone.
- The restraint to wait when action would cause harm.
- The decision to remain aligned even when no one is watching.

These small moments shape the current of a life.
You do not need to change everything overnight.
You need only choose the next aligned action, and then the next.

Still waters do not become still by force;
they become still by consistency.

YOUR PATH WILL WANDER — AND THAT IS PART OF THE WAY

No one walks in perfect balance.
You will drift. You will forget. You will falter.
There will be days when your courage softens, days when your compassion frays, days when truth feels heavy or inconvenient.

This does not place you outside the Way.
It simply means you are human.

The Way is not a straight line, but a river:
sometimes swift, sometimes shallow, sometimes clouded by storm.
The measure of a practitioner is not flawless discipline —
it is the willingness to return.

Return to stillness.
Return to integrity.
Return to the quiet knowing of what is right.

Every return strengthens the current.

ON HEALING, REPAIR, AND RENEWAL

Many who come to the Way do so carrying old wounds — betrayal, disappointment, loneliness, shame, anger, self-doubt, or the ache of relationships that have frayed or broken.

Let this be said clearly:

You are not beyond repair.
Your story is not fixed.
You have not failed simply because you have been hurt.

Healing is not linear.
It is not a single awakening, but many small softenings:

- Choosing truth after deceit.
- Choosing boundaries after chaos.
- Choosing self-respect after self-abandonment.
- Choosing patience while pain settles.
- Choosing compassion without losing firmness.

The Way invites you to meet yourself with honesty and dignity — not judgment, not avoidance, not perfectionism.

You cannot walk forward while carrying the illusion that you are unworthy of forward motion.

THE WAY IN RELATIONSHIPS

This Codex has given you a clear compass for connection:

TRUTH, HONOR, RESPONSIBILITY, COMPASSION, BALANCE, AND NO HARM.

These are not merely ideals.
They are the foundation upon which all healthy bonds — romantic, familial, platonic, communal — must rest.

Whether your path leads you into monogamy, polyamory, casual connection, or committed partnership, the question is never:

"Which structure is right?"

The question is always:

"Am I living this structure with integrity?"

And if the answer is no, the Way calls for alignment, not shame.

If repair is possible, seek repair.
If departure is needed, depart with dignity.
If renewal is available, welcome it with humility.

The Way does not punish.
It simply reveals where truth and kindness must flow again.

THE WAY IN A TURBULENT WORLD

We live in a time of constant noise — endless communication, fractured attention, performative conflict, and momentary connections dressed as depth.

To walk the Way today is to embody a rare steadiness:

- To be calm in a culture of reaction.
- To be honest in a culture of convenience.
- To be compassionate in a culture of judgment.
- To be resolute in a culture of avoidance.
- To be clear in a culture of ambiguity.

Still waters are not silent waters.
They are simply waters that refuse to be disturbed by every passing wind.

Your practice may not change the world at large — but it will change the world within your reach.

That is enough.

LIVING THE WAY, QUIETLY AND CONSISTENTLY

As you move beyond these pages, remember:

The Way does not demand extraordinary acts.
It asks only that you live your values in ordinary moments.

Begin your morning with intention.
Walk your day with awareness.
Close your evening with reflection.
Return to the river when you drift.
Treat each choice as a ripple.
And carry your strength with gentleness.

In time, you will notice the shift:
your reactions softening,
your clarity sharpening,
your relationships deepening,
your peace strengthening.

This is the quiet transformation the Way offers —
not a sudden blaze, but a steady flame.

A FINAL REFLECTION

If you have read this far, you have already begun.
The river is beneath your feet.
The current is waiting.

The Way of Still Waters is not a path you follow.
It is a path you become.

- Steel in your will.
  - Water in your heart.
  - Balance in your steps.

Walk gently.
Walk wisely.
Walk with courage.

And may your stillness carry you farther than force ever could.

THE DOCTOR — ON STARTING OVER

Starting over isn't a failure.

It's the universe tapping you on the shoulder and saying,

'Try again — you're not done yet.'

You're allowed to change direction,

to rewrite your story,

to become someone new without apologizing for who you were.

"Regeneration isn't just for Time Lords.

Every heart gets more than one beginning."

THE 11 STREAMS: SOURCES
AND SCOPE

While we touch on these in the core text, these notes are provided for those who wish to dig deeper into the main streams' original sources. Together, the real-world and fictional streams serve distinct but complementary roles within the Way: one grounding its ethics in lived human history; the other providing symbolic language that clarifies and reinforces those same principles without supplanting them. These references are provided for historical and philosophical context, not as prescriptive authorities, and are intended to support further study rather than define doctrine within The Way of Still Waters.

REAL-WORLD STREAMS

Several streams within The Way of Still Waters draw directly from historical philosophies, ethical traditions, and lived practices that developed within real cultures over extended periods of time. These real-world streams – including Stoicism, Taoism, Bushidō, chivalric ethics, and frontier guardianship traditions – are engaged as philosophical foundations rather than symbolic metaphors, offering tested frameworks for moral clarity, disciplined conduct, relational responsibility, and balanced action grounded in human experience.

The inclusion of these real-world streams does not present any single tradition as complete or infallible, nor does it require religious adherence, cultural adoption, or historical reenactment. Instead, each tradition is approached with discernment and respect, abstracted to its ethical principles and integrated into a unified framework oriented toward practical application, accountability, and compassion in modern life, in alignment with the Way's core commitments to truth, responsibility, balance, and non-harm.

The Taoist Stream of The Way of Still Waters draws philosophical inspiration from Taoism, an ancient Chinese tradition that emphasizes harmony with the natural order, balance through yielding, and action guided by timing rather than force. These teachings are employed to illuminate ethical patterns such as non-contention, adaptability, humility, and the cultivation of inner stillness amid change, rather than to prescribe metaphysical belief or religious practice. The Taoist Stream rejects passivity, fatalism, and withdrawal from responsibility, articulating instead an ethic of responsive wisdom, proportionate action, and alignment with life's natural rhythms.

For more information on Taoism, please refer to classical Taoist texts such as "Tao Te Ching", Zhuangzi, and modern interpretive works, including "The Tao of Pooh" by Benjamin Hoff.

The Stoic Stream of The Way of Still Waters draws philosophical inspiration from Stoicism, the Greco-Roman ethical tradition concerned with reasoned judgment, moral clarity, and resilience in the face of uncertainty. These teachings are used to clarify ethical patterns such as responsibility for one's actions, discernment between what can and cannot be controlled, and the cultivation of virtue independent of external outcomes, rather than to promote emotional suppression or rigid asceticism. The Stoic Stream rejects detachment from compassion and emphasizes steadiness, accountability, and principled action guided by reason and conscience.

For more information on Stoicism, please refer to foundational works such as "Meditations" (Marcus Aurelius), "Letters from a Stoic" (Seneca), and "Discourses" (Epictetus).

THE SAMURAI (BUSHIDŌ) STREAM

The Samurai Stream of The Way of Still Waters draws historical and philosophical inspiration from Bushidō, the ethical framework associated with Japan's samurai class, which emphasized honor, duty, restraint, and disciplined conduct. These principles are referenced to illuminate ethical patterns such as loyalty to conscience, self-mastery, and responsibility bound to action, rather than to endorse feudal hierarchy, martial dominance, or ritualized violence. The Samurai Stream rejects glorification of death, blind obedience, and rigid traditionalism, articulating instead an ethic of disciplined integrity, measured courage, and service governed by moral judgment.

For more information on Bushidō, please refer to historical and philosophical texts such as Hagakure, "The Book of Five Rings", and "Bushido: The Soul of Japan" (Nitobe).

THE KNIGHTLY / CHIVALRIC STREAM

The Knightly Stream of The Way of Still Waters draws historical inspiration from medieval European chivalry, a moral ideal that sought to bind strength to service, courage to mercy, and power to the protection of the vulnerable. These traditions are referenced to highlight ethical patterns such as honor expressed through conduct, restraint in the use of force, and responsibility toward those under one's care, rather than to promote romanticized warfare, social hierarchy, or aristocratic privilege. The Chivalric Stream rejects conquest, domination, and performative honor, articulating instead an ethic of service, humility, and compassion guided by conscience rather than status.

For more information on chivalry, please refer to medieval and scholarly works such as "The Book of Chivalry" (Geoffroi de Charny), "Le Morte d'Arthur" (Thomas Malory), and modern historical studies on medieval knighthood and chivalric ethics.

THE RANGER STREAM

The Ranger Stream of The Way of Still Waters draws historical and ethical inspiration from frontier guardianship roles found across cultures and periods, including border wardens, scouts, trackers, forest wardens, and coastal watchers tasked with early warning, protection, and vigilance at the edges of settled society. These roles are referenced to illuminate ethical patterns such as situational awareness, restraint, stewardship, and responsibility grounded in competence rather than authority, or to promote narrative identity or romanticized frontier mythology. The Ranger Stream rejects vigilantism, conquest, and "lone-wolf" power narratives, articulating instead a practical ethic of discernment, accountability, and quiet guardianship intended for real-world application.

For more information on historical frontier guardianship and ranger archetypes, please refer to historical studies of border wardens, scouts, and wilderness stewardship, as well as literary works such as The Lord of the Rings by J. R. R. Tolkien.

FICTIONAL STREAMS

Several streams within The Way of Still Waters draw symbolic inspiration from fictional cultures and characters found in modern science fiction and mythic storytelling, which are referenced solely as illustrative metaphors for ethical patterns rather than as narrative identities, belief systems, or prescriptions for role-play. These fictional sources are used to highlight recurring moral themes – such as disciplined restraint, compassion under pressure, honor-bound responsibility, guardianship without domination, and resistance to cruelty – that echo ethical principles found across real-world philosophies, histories, and lived human experience.

The inclusion of these fictional streams does not endorse imitation, cosplay, fandom identity, or the literal adoption of fictional doctrines, hierarchies, or conflicts, nor does it romanticize violence, vigilantism, conquest, or authoritarian power. Instead, each stream is abstracted to its ethical essence and integrated into a practical framework of accountability, discernment, and compassion, intended for real-world application in modern life. Fictional references serve as shared symbolic language only, offering clarity and resonance while remaining firmly subordinate to the Way's core commitment to truth, responsibility, balance, and non-harm.

THE JEDI STREAM

The Jedi Stream of The Way of Still Waters draws symbolic inspiration from the fictional Jedi Order depicted in Star Wars, which portrays guardians who combine disciplined power, emotional restraint, and service to a larger moral good. These references are employed solely as illustrative metaphors for ethical patterns – such as self-mastery, responsibility in the use of power, and resistance to fear and cruelty – rather than as narrative identities, belief systems, or prescriptions for role-play. The Jedi Stream does not endorse dogma, detachment from humanity, or authoritarian moral certainty, but instead distills a practical ethic of restraint, accountability, and compassionate action intended for real-world application.

For more information on the Jedi, please refer to the various media within the Star Wars universe, which began with the 1977 film created by George Lucas.

THE MANDALORIAN STREAM

The Mandalorian Stream of The Way of Still Waters draws symbolic inspiration from Mandalorian culture as depicted in Star Wars media, emphasizing themes of personal creed, chosen family, responsibility bound to identity, and honor expressed through conduct rather than status. These elements are referenced solely as metaphors to illuminate ethical commitments – such as keeping one's word, protecting those under one's care, and accepting the weight of chosen obligations – rather than as endorsements of fictional hierarchies, warrior cultures, or role-play identities. The Mandalorian Stream explicitly rejects conquest, tribalism, and glorified violence, articulating instead a grounded ethic of responsibility, loyalty tempered by conscience, and strength exercised in service of others.

For more information on Mandalorians, please refer to the various media within the Star Wars universe, which began with the 1977 film created by George Lucas.

THE KLINGON STREAM

The Klingon Stream of The Way of Still Waters draws symbolic inspiration from Klingon culture as portrayed in Star Trek, using it as a metaphorical lens for examining honor, forthrightness, courage, and integrity in the face of adversity. These references are employed to highlight ethical clarity, truthfulness, and the refusal to live in self-deception, not to promote aggression, domination, or rigid warrior identity. The Klingon Stream rejects brutality, pride without restraint, and conflict for its own sake, refining instead an ethic in which honor is measured by accountability, sincerity, and the courage to face reality without evasion.

For more information on Klingon culture, please refer to the Star Trek television series and related media, first introduced by Gene Roddenberry in 1966.

THE MINBARI STREAM

The Minbari Stream of The Way of Still Waters draws symbolic inspiration from Minbari philosophy as depicted in Babylon 5, particularly its emphasis on spiritual discipline, humility before truth, patience, and long-view awareness of consequence. These references are used solely as metaphors for ethical reflection and inner stillness, not as spiritual doctrine, belief system, or fictional cosmology. The Minbari Stream does not promote mysticism, prophecy, or withdrawal from responsibility, but instead articulates a practical ethic of contemplation, restraint, and alignment with truth prior to action.

For more information on the Minbari, please refer to the television series Babylon 5, created by J. Michael Straczynski and first aired in 1994.

THE ANLA'SHOK STREAM

The Anla'Shok Stream of The Way of Still Waters draws symbolic inspiration from the Anla'Shok (Rangers) of Babylon 5, depicted as a watchful order committed to standing between chaos and peace through sacrifice, vigilance, and moral courage. These references serve as illustrative metaphors for ethical guardianship and preventative action, not as prescriptions for militarized identity, secrecy, or hierarchical command. The Anla'Shok Stream rejects glorification of sacrifice for its own sake and instead emphasizes discernment, accountability, and the willingness to act when harm threatens, always in service of balance rather than domination.

For more information on the Anla'Shok (Rangers), please refer to the television series Babylon 5, created by J. Michael Straczynski and first aired in 1994.

THE DOCTOR STREAM

The Doctor Stream of The Way of Still Waters draws symbolic inspiration from the character known as the Doctor in Doctor Who, using this figure as a metaphor for an ethical archetype that values intellect, compassion, restraint, and fierce opposition to cruelty. These references are employed to illuminate moral patterns – such as choosing kindness under pressure, protecting life without becoming its master, and holding power accountable to conscience – rather than to encourage imitation, identity adoption, or narrative role-play. The Doctor Stream explicitly rejects savior complexes and moral exceptionalism, articulating instead an ethic of humility, responsibility, and courage guided by empathy and reason.

For more information on The Doctor, please refer to the BBC's television series Doctor Who, originally created by Sydney Newman, C. E. Webber, and Donald Wilson in 1963.

INSPIRATIONAL QUOTATIONS

STOICISM

INNER SOVEREIGNTY • EMOTIONAL DISCIPLINE • COURAGE IN STILLNESS

"You have power over your mind — not outside events. Realize this, and you will find strength."
– Marcus Aurelius
Way Connection: Control the oar, not the river.

"It is not things that disturb us, but our judgments about things."
– Epictetus
Way Connection: Interpretation precedes reaction.

"Sometimes even to live is an act of courage."
– Seneca
Way Connection: Remaining still is sometimes the boldest act.

"Waste no more time arguing what a good man should be. Be one."
– Marcus Aurelius
Way Connection: Virtue is enacted, not theorized.

"How long are you going to wait before you demand the best for yourself?"
– Epictetus
Way Connection: The Way begins with self-accountability.

"Dwell on the beauty of life. Watch the stars, and see yourself running with them."
– Marcus Aurelius
Way Connection: Still Waters reflect the sky.

TAOISM

FLOW • NON-FORCING • WATER AS MASTER TEACHER

"Nothing in the world is as soft and yielding as water, yet nothing can surpass it in overcoming the hard."
– Lao Tzu, Tao Te Ching
Way Connection: The Way conquers by flowing, not clashing.

"The soft overcomes the hard; the gentle overcomes the rigid."
– Lao Tzu, Tao Te Ching
Way Connection: Gentleness is a form of strategy.

"The highest good is like water. Water benefits all things and does not compete."
– Lao Tzu, Tao Te Ching
Way Connection: Serve quietly, without seeking dominance.

"When nothing is done, nothing is left undone."
– Lao Tzu, Tao Te Ching
Way Connection: Non-forcing creates natural resolutions.

"Those who flow as life flows know they need no other force."
– Lao Tzu, Tao Te Ching
Way Connection: Alignment replaces opposition.

"To understand the limitation of things, desire them."
– Lao Tzu, Tao Te Ching
Way Connection: Awareness dissolves attachment.

BUSHIDŌ (SAMURAI)

RECTITUDE • DUTY • HONOR CARRIED QUIETLY

"Rectitude is the power of deciding upon a certain course of conduct in
accordance with reason, without wavering."
– Nitobe
Way Connection: Choose your shoreline; stay to it.

"Courage is doing what is right."
– Bushidō precept
Way Connection: Courage without moral alignment is chaos.

"Rectitude, courage, benevolence, politeness, sincerity, honor, loyalty,
self-control — these are the virtues of Bushidō."
Way Connection: A direct ancestor to The Way's Twelve.

"The sword is the soul of the samurai."
– Traditional teaching
Way Connection: Tools reflect the heart of the one who wields them.

"It is not the path that is difficult; it is the difficulties that become the
path."
– Samurai saying
Way Connection: Obstacles shape practice.

"A samurai's life is the expression of a disciplined heart."
Way Connection: Discipline is the steady current under the surface.

CHIVALRY (KNIGHTLY CODES)

PROTECTION • DUTY TO THE WEAK • COURTESY AS STRENGTH

"True chivalry protects the feeble and serves womankind..."
– Louisa May Alcott
Way Connection: Honor is measured by who you defend.

"To protect the weak and defenseless; to give succor to widows and orphans."
– Knightly Oath summary
Way Connection: The strong are guardians, not predators.

"Above all, he must uphold the weak; thus should a knight rule himself."
Way Connection: Self-mastery expresses itself as service.

"Live pure, speak true, right wrong."
– Tennyson, *Idylls of the King*
Way Connection: Purity, honesty, and justice echo The Way.

"Strength is given to you not to rule over others, but to shield them."
– Chivalric principle
Way Connection: Power flows outward, not upward.

"Honor is loyalty to what is right."
Way Connection: Honor is an action, not a status.

THE JEDI CODE

CALM • CLARITY • SERVICE OVER EGO

"There is no emotion, there is peace."
Way Connection: Emotion acknowledged, not enthroned.

"There is no ignorance, there is knowledge."
Way Connection: Learn before acting.

"There is no passion, there is serenity."
Way Connection: Intensity without compulsion.

"There is no chaos, there is harmony."
Way Connection: Find the pattern beneath disturbance.

"Your focus determines your reality."
– Jedi teaching
Way Connection: Attention shapes outcome.

"The greatest teacher, failure is."
– Yoda
Way Connection: Every misstep is part of the riverbed.

THE MANDALORIAN CREED

CREED AS IDENTITY • FOUND-FAMILY DUTY • STEADFAST RESOLVE

"And the words of the Creed shall be forever forged in my heart. This is The Way."
Way Connection: The Way is carried internally.

"By creed... you are as its father. This is The Way."
Way Connection: Duty chosen is duty kept.

"Mandalorian is not a race; it's a creed."
Way Connection: The Way is chosen, not inherited.

"Weapons are part of my religion."
– Din Djarin
Way Connection: Tools are extensions of commitment.

"Honor the bargain. Honor the rescue. Honor the foundling."
Way Connection: Duty flows downward to the vulnerable.

"This is The Way."
Way Connection: A whole ethos distilled into one line: chosen, lived, embodied.

KLINGON HONOR CODE

INTEGRITY • VALOR • CLEAN CONDUCT EVEN IN CONFLICT

"There is no honor in attacking the weak."
Way Connection: Strength bows to restraint.

"Honor is more important than life."
Way Connection: Survival without integrity is failure.

"One does not achieve honor while acting dishonorably."
Way Connection: Means must match the claimed virtue.

"A warrior does not let fear control his actions."
Way Connection: Courage is a choice, not a feeling.

"Great men do not seek war, but when it comes, they face it boldly."
Way Connection: Conflict is engaged with clean intent.

"Today is a good day to die."
(proper context: readiness, not fatalism)
Way Connection: Acceptance of mortality clarifies purpose.

MINBARI SPIRITUAL ETHOS

FAITH • REASON • LIFE AS SACRED

"Faith manages."
– Delenn
Way Connection: Release what lies beyond control.

"Faith and reason are the shoes on your feet. Travel further with both."
Way Connection: Balance of intuition and logic.

"This is my cause — life! One life or a billion, it's all the same!"
Way Connection: Scale does not change worth.

"The universe speaks in subtle truths."
– Minbari teaching
Way Connection: Awareness is a discipline.

"Understanding is a three-edged sword: your side, their side, and the truth."
– Vorlon/Minbari maxim
Way Connection: Truth floats between perspectives.

"All life is sacred. No greater responsibility exists than to protect it."
Way Connection: Sacredness = duty.

ANLA'SHOK / RANGERS

GUARDIANSHIP • BALANCE • SERVICE IN THE SHADOWS

"We walk in dark places no others will enter. We stand on the bridge and no one may pass."
Way Connection: Guardians at the river's edge.

"We are Grey. We stand between the darkness and the light."
Way Connection: The Way rejects extremes; holds center.

"We do not retreat."
Way Connection: Once committed, stay.

"You carry the message: Not the person."
– Ranger teaching
Way Connection: Ego must not compromise mission.

"The avalanche has already started. It is too late for the pebbles to vote."
– Kosh
Way Connection: Accept the river once it moves.

"There is always hope. Only the end of time is truly hopeless."
Way Connection: Persistence is an act of faith.

DOCTOR WHO ETHIC OF KINDNESS

*KINDNESS AS DISCIPLINE • MORAL COURAGE • THE DECENCY
IMPERATIVE*

"Never be cruel. Never be cowardly."
Way Connection: Foundational prohibitions.

"Hate is always foolish, and love is always wise."
Way Connection: Choose the wiser emotion.

**"I do what I do because it's right, because it's decent. And above all, it's
kind."**
Way Connection: Action = virtue + decency + kindness.

"Always try to be nice, but never fail to be kind."
Way Connection: Kindness is not optional.

**"Courage isn't just a matter of not being frightened. It's being afraid and
doing what you have to do anyway."**
– Third Doctor
Way Connection: Feelings don't dictate duty.

**"Never ignore a coincidence. Unless you're busy, then always ignore a
coincidence."**
– Eleventh Doctor
Way Connection: Stay aware, but stay practical.

APPENDIX I: FOUNDATIONS OF THE WAY (Q1-20)

1. *What is The Way of Still Waters in one sentence?*

The Way of Still Waters is a living code of honour and Balance—a commitment to honesty, courage, compassion, and clarity, even when it costs you.

2. *Is this a religion, fandom thing, or self-help system?*

It is a code of practice, not a religion. The imagery is symbolic; the discipline is personal and lived.

3. *What are the Original Twelve virtues?*

Fair Play, Nobility, Valour, Courtesy, Fidelity, Duty, Integrity, Respect, Courage, Honour, Compassion, Honesty, Loyalty.

4. *What are the Refined Nine?*

Courtesy, Honour, Courage, Integrity, Duty, Compassion, Wisdom, Humility, and Balance (the unifying principle).

5. *What does "Still Waters" mean?*

It means choosing responses from clarity, not emotional turbulence.

6. *Does following The Way mean being passive?*

No. Stillness is controlled strength, not surrender.

7. *How does The Way relate to Doctor Who's teachings?*

Both insist that kindness and courage together define right action, especially "in extremis."

8. *Can anyone use The Way?*

Yes. It complements any belief system rooted in virtue.

9. *How is this different from generic "be good" advice?*

It is structured, virtue-based, and focused on courage + compassion in difficult choices.

10. *What is the Still Waters Test?*

Is it honest, fair, and kind—and would I accept its ripple if known?

11. *What counts as cheating?*

Any secret betrayal of romantic or emotional fidelity.

12. *Is emotional cheating real cheating?*

Yes. Secret emotional intimacy breaks integrity.

13. *When does flirting become cheating?*

When it is hidden or pursued as mutual attraction.

14. *What about online sexual interactions?*

Sexual secrecy = betrayal, regardless of medium.

15. *Can cheating be accidental?*

No. Betrayal requires at least one conscious choice.

16. *How do I know if my partner respects me?*

Look for consistency, accountability, and care.

17. **What if my partner avoids feelings?**

Avoidance blocks intimacy; courage demands truthful connection.

18. **How does The Way view situationships?**

Clarity and honesty are required; ambiguity to avoid responsibility is misaligned.

19. **How do I date honourably?**

State your intentions honestly; exit cleanly when misaligned.

20. **What if I'm "too much"?**

You are only "too much" for someone who wants to invest less than you.

APPENDIX II: CHEATING, FIDELITY, AND ROMANTIC BONDS (Q21-60)

21. *What counts as emotional cheating?*

Any secret emotional intimacy that replaces or competes with a committed bond.

22. *Why is secrecy the core betrayal?*

Because secrecy breaks Integrity, the spine virtue of The Way.

23. *Can a relationship recover from cheating?*

Yes, but only with full truth, accountability, and long-term changed behavior.

24. *What is the first step after discovering betrayal?*

Do not self-blame. Seek clarity before making decisions.

25. *How should one who betrayed begin repair?*

By owning the harm completely without minimizing.

26. *Is flirting always a threat?*

Flirting becomes a threat when it is hidden or pursued.

27. *Can online intimacy be worse than physical cheating?*

Sometimes—because emotional replacement often cuts deeper.

28. *How does The Way define romantic loyalty?*

Loyalty in action, speech, attention, and emotional investment.

29. *What if my partner and I have different definitions of cheating?*

Discuss, define, and agree on boundaries explicitly.

30. *Is jealousy always unhealthy?*

No. It is a signal, not a verdict. Its meaning must be explored.

31. *When does jealousy reveal incompatibility?*

When needs for transparency differ beyond negotiation.

32. *What if my partner dismisses my concerns?*

Dismissal without examination is misaligned with Respect and Courtesy.

33. *How does The Way approach mismatched desire?*

With compassion, open discussion, and creative compromise.

34. *What if compromise is impossible?*

Then the relationship may not be viable long-term.

35. *How do I communicate hurt without causing harm?*

Describe impact, not character. Stay anchored in truth.

36. *What if we argue constantly?*

Look beneath patterns: unmet needs, poor communication, or misalignment.

37. *How do I keep relationship conflicts aligned with The Way?*

Avoid contempt, cruelty, and stonewalling; uphold honesty and care.

38. *What if they withdraw instead of discussing?*

Agree on a pause with a return time; refusal to return is avoidance.

39. *When should I leave a romantic relationship?*

When staying requires self-betrayal or enduring continuous harm.

40. *What if I fear being alone?*

Aloneness is a season; self-betrayal is a wound. Choose healing.

41. *How does The Way guide new relationships?*

Go slow, be clear, observe patterns, prioritize integrity.

42. *How do I avoid repeating old mistakes?*

Reflect, name patterns, set boundaries, act intentionally.

43. *How do I date while healing?*

Honestly name your stage; move at a pace grounded in clarity.

44. *What does care look like in alignment with The Way?*

Attentive listening, consistent effort, kindness with boundaries.

45. *What if my partner hides their phone?*

Secrecy signals misalignment; transparency signals care.

46. *How do I handle attraction to someone else?*

Acknowledge it privately, examine its meaning, protect your bond.

47. *What if the attraction reveals unmet needs?*

Bring those needs forward in honest discussion.

48. *How do I stay loving during conflict?*

Stay rooted in compassion and truth, not ego or victory.

49. *What if I'm losing feelings?*

Explore why; feelings often follow connection and effort.

50. *Can love be rebuilt?*

Yes—through shared effort, vulnerability, and intentional time.

51. *When is love no longer healthy?*

When it consistently erodes your dignity, peace, or integrity.

52. *How do I recognize genuine remorse?*

Remorse takes the shape of change, not just regret.

53. *How do I foster trust with a new partner?*

Consistency, transparency, communication.

54. *What if my partner's friends disrespect me?*

Your partner must address it; loyalty includes advocacy.

55. *How do I handle incompatibility in emotional expression?*

Learn each other's "languages" with patience.

56. *What if their "language" harms me?*

Then adaptation is needed from them too; love is reciprocal.

57. *Does The Way allow second chances?*

Yes—once, if change is real.

58. *What is required for a true second chance?*

Firm boundaries, clear agreements, consistent actions.

59. *What if trust never returns?*

Then the relationship cannot thrive; leaving may be most aligned.

60. *How do I end a romantic bond with honour?*

With honesty, clarity, compassion, and a clean exit.

APPENDIX III: FAMILY, FRIENDSHIP, AND SOCIAL BONDS (Q61-100)

61. *How do I handle parents who still treat me like a child?*

With courtesy and clarity: "I appreciate your care, but this decision is mine."

62. *What if my family dismisses my boundaries?*

Boundaries don't require agreement—only respect.

63. *How do I deal with a sibling who competes with me?*

Refuse the game; do not feed comparison.

64. *What if my family pressures me to interact with a toxic relative?*

Family is not an override for self-preservation.

65. *How do I handle family rejecting my identity?*

Self-betrayal is never the virtuous option.

66. *What if I'm the family peacekeeper and exhausted?*

Your role is not your identity; step back.

67. *How do I respond when an estranged family member wants back in?*

Check for accountability, change, and mutual respect.

68. *What if my family drains me even though I love them?*

Shorten visits, set limits, schedule recovery.

69. *Am I wrong for becoming the "black sheep"?*

Often the "black sheep" is simply the one who stops pretending.

70. *What if loyalty to family conflicts with integrity?*

Integrity outranks blind loyalty in The Way.

71. *How do I end a friendship without cruelty?*

Clear truth, soft tone, clean exit.

72. *What if a friend only comes around when they need something?*

Recognize it as transactional; adjust closeness.

73. *How do I handle friends who guilt-trip me?*

State: "Guilt won't guide my choices. Let's talk honestly."

74. *What if a friend plays the victim constantly?*

Offer compassion, not rescue; set boundaries.

75. *What if someone weaponizes my vulnerabilities?*

That is a trust breach; distance is warranted.

76. *What if people punish me with silence?*

Clarify once; do not chase manipulation.

77. *How do I know when a friendship is over?*

When self-betrayal becomes the entry fee.

78. *How do I stay kind with people who hurt me?*

Kindness does not require access.

79. *How do I deal with someone who interrupts constantly?*

State the pattern; request space; disengage if ignored.

80. *How do I handle friends who minimize my achievements?*

Don't shrink; celebrate anyway; limit sharing with them.

81. *What if someone always blames circumstances, never choices?*

Accountability is necessary for a healthy bond.

82. *How do I respond to someone who lies about small things?*

Small lies are practice for bigger ones.

83. *What if someone treats strangers better than me?*

Masks slip where comfort grows; note the real behavior.

84. *What if I feel responsible for everyone's feelings?*

You are responsible for conduct, not for emotional weather.

85. *How do I stop rescuing people?*

Recognize enabling as disguised control; release responsibility.

86. *What if someone gets defensive when I express needs?*

State calmly; patterns reveal compatibility.

87. *How do I deal with people who expect endless forgiveness?*

Forgiveness is a gift, not an obligation.

88. *What if people take my silence as agreement?*

Speak a single clarifying sentence; do not argue.

89. *How do I stay aligned around toxic people?*

Minimum exposure, maximum clarity, zero self-betrayal.

90. *What if someone's chaos becomes my burden?*

You can care without carrying.

91. *How do I handle a friend who chronically cancels?*

Reduce investment; honor your time.

92. *What if someone's moods dominate the room?*

Their emotional storms are not your responsibility.

93. *How do I maintain dignity with disrespectful family?*

State boundaries firmly; limit contact if needed.

94. *What if I can't fix family conflict?*

You are responsible for clarity, not outcomes.

95. *What does healthy reciprocity look like?*

Shared effort, mutual care, Balanced listening.

96. *How do I handle someone who refuses apology?*

Truth, boundaries, and distance.

97. *What if they apologize but never change?*

Pattern outweighs apology.

98. *How do I stop feeling guilty for protecting myself?*

Remember: self-preservation is a virtue, not selfishness.

99. *What if they won't hear my truth?*

Say it once with clarity; silence after that is not surrender—it's wisdom.

100. *How do I walk away with honour?*

With truth, compassion, and the refusal to speak cruelty.

APPENDIX IV: MARRIAGE, DEEP RELATIONSHIPS, AND CONFLICT (Q101-140)

101. *What if marriage starts feeling like a roommate situation?*

It is a warning sign. Name it gently and pursue reconnection intentionally.

102. *How do we rebuild closeness?*

Rituals, shared time, vulnerability, and honest check-ins.

103. *Can constant small arguments signal deeper issues?*

Yes—often unmet needs or unfair labor distribution.

104. *How do we address the "invisible labor" imBalance?*

List duties, redistribute fairly, revisit regularly.

105. *What if my spouse shuts down during conflict?*

Use time-outs with agreed return times; stonewalling is misalignment.

106. *How do we resolve mismatched values?*

Respect is mandatory; value clashes that deny dignity are irreconcilable.

107. *What about financial conflict?*

Transparency, honesty, shared planning—no hidden debts or spending.

108. *How do I address secretive behavior in marriage?*

Secrets destroy integrity; address immediately and directly.

109. *What if my partner gaslights me?*

Gaslighting violates truth and honor; seek support and redraw boundaries.

110. *How do we handle mismatched intimacy?*

Communicate openly, seek compromise, and consider counseling.

111. *What if compromise feels impossible?*

Then deeper misalignment may exist; explore therapy and clarity.

112. *How do I maintain respect in heated arguments?*

Avoid contempt, insults, and cruelty; stay anchored in truth.

113. *How do we practice repair after conflict?*

Own actions, validate feelings, adjust behavior.

114. *What if apologies come without change?*

Then it is not remorse—only regret.

115. *How do I rebuild trust in marriage?*

Transparency, consistency, patience.

116. *What if trust never returns?*

A bond cannot thrive without trust; ending may be aligned.

117. *How does The Way treat long-term loyalty?*

Chosen loyalty is honored; blind loyalty is not.

118. *What if my partner belittles my feelings?*

Belittling is disrespect; commit to discussion or seek counseling.

119. *Can love survive betrayal?*

Yes, but only with radical honesty and deep accountability.

120. *How do I know if my spouse respects me?*

Through patterns of listening, fairness, and shared responsibility.

121. *What if my partner refuses all growth?*

Invite, discuss, reflect; refusal may signal incompatibility.

122. *How do we handle different communication styles?*

Learn each other's rhythms; meet in the middle.

123. *What if conflict becomes our normal?*

Chronic conflict signals unmet needs or mismatched expectations.

124. *How do I express needs without attacking?*

Use impact statements: "When X happens, I feel Y."

125. *What if they always interpret needs as criticism?*

That signals emotional defensiveness needing support.

126. *How do we reconnect after emotional distance?*

Small consistent acts, curiosity, presence.

127. *What if therapy is refused?*

Try individual therapy; consider if refusal indicates a deeper issue.

128. *How do I leave a marriage with honor?*

With truth, dignity, compassion—and no cruelty.

129. *What if the marriage ended but resentment lingers?*

Resentment is unprocessed pain; process through reflection and healing.

130. *How do I navigate co-parenting after separation?*

Prioritize children's well-being over ego battles.

131. *How do I stay fair in divorce?*

Honor agreements, avoid vindictiveness, maintain clarity.

132. *What if my ex continues conflict cycles?*

Set firm communication boundaries—written only if needed.

133. *Should I forgive an ex?*

Forgive internally for peace, not for re-entry.

134. *How do I stop repeating marriage mistakes?*

Reflect, identify patterns, seek self-mastery.

135. *What if my partner weaponizes therapy language?*

Clarify intentions; seek neutral facilitation.

136. *How do I stay emotionally safe in conflict?*

Take breaks, breathe, avoid escalation.

137. *What if I fear my partner's anger?*

Anger that instills fear signals potential abuse—seek support.

138. *How do I know the difference between incompatibility and burnout?*

Burnout heals with rest; incompatibility stays despite effort.

139. *How do I keep love alive long-term?*

Curiosity, kindness, shared purpose, and continuous small acts.

140. *What if leaving is the only aligned choice?*

Leave with honesty and compassion; alignment sometimes requires endings.

APPENDIX V: CAREER, DAILY LIFE, AND SELF-DEVELOPMENT (Q141-180)

141. *How do I live The Way in a toxic workplace?*

Remain courteous, avoid cruelty, document issues, and plan an exit that preserves integrity.

142. *What if my boss pressures me to lie?*

Decline respectfully: honesty is non-negotiable in The Way.

143. *How do I deal with gossip at work?*

Withdraw from gossip; redirect conversations toward clarity and fairness.

144. *What if my work is never recognized?*

Self-advocate calmly and document contributions.

145. *How do I prevent burnout?*

Set boundaries, rest deliberately, learn to say no.

146. *How does The Way view ambition?*

Ambition aligned with integrity is noble; ambition fueled by ego is misalignment.

147. *How do I lead others with honour?*

Serve, communicate clearly, and uplift those you lead.

148. *What if coworkers exploit my kindness?*

Kindness requires boundaries; say no when overburdened.

149. *When should I leave a job?*

When staying requires self-betrayal or participation in harm.

150. *How do I remain ethical in competitive industries?*

Choose truth, fairness, and transparency—even if it costs opportunities.

151. *How do I Balance work with personal life?*

Create sacred boundaries; honour your wholeness.

152. *How do I stay calm under pressure?*

Pause, breathe, and act after the "water" settles.

153. *How do I practice humility in my career?*

Recognize strengths without arrogance and weaknesses without shame.

154. *What if coworkers dislike my calmness?*

Your calm reveals their turbulence; stay aligned.

155. *How do I handle workplace injustice?*

Expose truth through correct channels; refuse complicity.

156. *How does The Way view promotions?*

Accept them with humility; lead with integrity.

157. *How do I respond to a hostile environment?*

Minimize exposure and protect your dignity.

158. *What if someone takes credit for my work?*

Document, clarify facts, and involve leadership.

159. *How do I nurture creativity while living The Way?*

Create from clarity—not ego, fear, or comparison.

160. *How do I handle feeling undervalued?*

Re-evaluate your environment; seek spaces that honour you.

161. *How do I practice The Way in everyday decisions?*

Ask: Is it honest? Is it fair? Is it kind? Can I live with the ripple?

162. *How do I stop people-pleasing?*

Replace approval-seeking with integrity-seeking.

163. *How do I remain compassionate without being drained?*

Compassion with boundaries prevents depletion.

164. *How do I stay disciplined?*

Break tasks into small steps; honour commitments to yourself.

165. *How do I navigate conflict with grace?*

Lead with truth, avoid cruelty, maintain clarity.

166. *What if I dread daily responsibilities?*

Courage is action despite discomfort; start small.

167. *How do I know if I am aligned with The Way?*

Your choices feel clear, consistent, and self-respecting.

168. *How do I handle envy of others' success?*

Let envy become curiosity and motivation, not bitterness.

169. *How do I focus in a chaotic world?*

Limit noise, cultivate stillness, practice presence.

170. *What if I feel stagnant?*

Seek new learning, reflection, or challenges.

171. *How do I develop wisdom?*

Observe without reacting; learn from every outcome.

172. *How do I avoid emotional reactivity?*

Pause, breathe, name the emotion, choose your response.

173. *How do I improve my boundaries?*

State them simply, uphold them consistently.

174. *How do I practice courage daily?*

Do one small hard thing each day.

175. *How do I avoid judging others harshly?*

Remember the code is a mirror, not a hammer.

176. *What if self-doubt overwhelms me?*

Recall your virtues; take small aligned actions.

177. *How do I practice self-respect?*

Treat yourself as someone whose well-being matters.

178. *How do I live with purpose?*

Follow what brings clarity, service, courage, and compassion.

179. *How do I know if I'm growing?*

Patterns change, reactions soften, boundaries strengthen.

180. *How do I stay aligned when tired or stressed?*

Simplify: do no harm, tell no lies, betray no part of yourself.

APPENDIX VI: GENERAL TEACHINGS AND THE DAILY LIVING OF THE WAY (Q181-200)

181. *Is it ever wrong to be kind?*

Kindness is never wrong, but unbounded kindness can become self-harm. Kindness must be paired with wisdom.

182. *How do I stop repeating unhealthy cycles?*

Identify the trigger, understand the root, choose different actions, and remain consistent.

183. *What if people misunderstand my intentions?*

Clarify once calmly; repeated misunderstanding is their narrative, not your responsibility.

184. *How do I respond to disrespect while staying calm?*

Stay steady, state the boundary, and refuse cruelty.

185. *What if silence is taken as agreement?*

Use simple clarification: "I see it differently." You do not need a debate.

186. *How do I stop caring about what others think?*

Shift your focus to: "Would the version of me I admire approve of this choice?"

187. *How do I build resilience?*

Resilience grows through consistent aligned actions, not avoidance.

188. *How do I deal with regret?*

Regret is a teacher—extract the lesson, apply it, and let go.

189. *How do I stay hopeful when the world feels dark?*

Look for small acts of good, create small acts of good, and anchor yourself in purpose.

190. *Do I have to explain my boundaries?*

No. Boundaries require clarity, not justification.

191. *How do I know if someone is safe to trust?*

Watch words under ease and actions under pressure.

192. *How do I stay aligned in a selfish world?*

Choose integrity even when the world does not reward it.

193. *How do I handle people exploiting my kindness?*

Be kind with boundaries; refuse exploitation without cruelty.

194. *How do I find my purpose?*

Follow curiosity, service, and what strengthens your courage and compassion.

195. *How do I move on from grief?*

Let grief flow without rushing it. Healing is not forgetting—it's integrating.

196. *How do I stop living in the past?*

Process, extract meaning, and deliberately shift identity toward who you are becoming.

197. *How do I protect my peace?*

Limit chaos, say no often, guard your emotional space.

198. *What if I keep attracting conflict?*

Examine boundaries, communication habits, and emotional patterns.

199. *What if I am afraid of change?*

Change is the river of life; resisting it causes suffering. Flow with awareness.

200. *How do I live The Way every day?*

Begin each morning with intention. Choose one virtue as your guide. Act with honesty, compassion, courage, and clarity. Reflect at night: Where did I align? Where can I improve? Return to the water, again and again, choosing The Way with each small act.

www.ingramcontent.com/pod-product-compliance
Lightning Source LLC
Chambersburg PA
CBHW052111030426

42335CB00025B/2940